Modern Australian Painting, 1970/1975

1 SYDNEY BALL
Cirondo Yellow (1974)
244 x 244 cms
Enamel and acrylic on cotton duck
Collection: Mr & Mrs G. O'Neill, Sydney
Photograph: Stan Ciccone, Sydney

MODERN AUSTRALIAN PAINTING, 1970/1975

Kym Bonython

Elwyn Lynn

 RIGBY

National Library of Australia
Cataloguing-in-Publication entry:

Modern Australian Painting, 1970/1975
  Index
  ISBN 0 7270 0087 X
  1. Paintings, Australian I. Bonython, Kym, comp.
  II. Lynn, Elwyn, ed.

  759.994

Rigby Limited • Adelaide • Sydney
Melbourne • Brisbane • Perth
First published 1976
Wholly designed and set up in Australia
Printed in Hong Kong

Contents

Introduction

In his lecture, "The Shape of Colour," given in various places in Australia in 1973, Patrick Heron made large claims for the act of painting; indeed, considering the climate of the times, seemingly exaggerated ones. He said, "I am saying that painting organises our sight, dictates the way we see everything we do see—which means nothing less than our entire environment. Painting alters the look of the world for us. I am not talking now of our practical vision . . . I am referring, on the contrary, to our contemplative vision, to the sort of seeing we employ the moment we start to think about 'the look of' a thing—of anything, in fact, that comes within our visual range . . .

"Painting's most potent discoveries . . . have all been arrived at by the most stunningly economical means—namely, the staining and marking with pigments of a two-dimensional flat surface bounded by two vertical and two horizontal edges."

Such a potent declaration about those simple marks, scratches, notations, signs, symbols, outlines, and smudges that have emanated magic since the times of the cave-dwellers affronted some who believed that art, having become too retinal and self-indulgent, needed a dose of Marcel Duchamp's cerebral self-denial; it affronted those who believed that the apotheosis of colour was a hankering after false gods and it affronted those who had been persuaded by various protagonists, always with their burial spades at the ready, that painting was dead. If not dead, it was but a pale, feeble shadow of its former self, more likely to arouse shivers of distaste than instant rapture.

Balanced commentators take a different view; John A. Walker, writing on what we may call the New Realism and Lyrical Abstraction, declares in his *Art Since Pop*: "Pundits have informed us that painting is dead; but perversely its corpse will not rest. However, if reviving past styles is a sign of decadence, then the paintings which the American artists David Diao, Robert Duran, Alan Shields, Ken Showell, James Sullivan, David Cummings, Donald Lewallen and others produced at the end of the 1960's must be counted as decadent: they reappraise the Abstract Expressionism of the 1950's and its European equivalent, *art informel*."

The entrance of the art grave-digger is a recent and peculiar phenomenon: articulate morticians who will both dig the grave and read a persuasive burial service abound. They do it so skilfully that few want to follow in the steps of their ancestors. As a result the expressionist tends to bridle the fury or ecstasy of his brush; the realist feels guilty about his lack of concern for those who dwell in the slum houses he depicts; and the pure abstractionist wonders whether he is an escapee from the real world.

To the art commentator who sees recent art history as a succession of burial mounds, the work and artists of any previous decade are dated, spent, irrelevant, and, if of any interest, just quaint, for our morticians are great dividers of artists and art into generations and short-lived periods. The decade, give or take a few years, becomes a kind of cultural division; what is new (and approved) in the 1960s is said to be the art of the 1960s; it is naturally expected that there will be an art (new and approved) that will be the art of the 1970s. Along with this goes the corollary that there are art gallery directors, critics, magazines, and publishers who made their contributions in the 1950s and 1960s and, as such, are unfit for the 1970s! The heralds of the new always blow a confident blast for the future and, almost simultaneously, a lament for the past, or at least a dirge for those who have made their contribution. Every decade most of the art world is supposed to lie down and declare itself defunct!

Consequently it is as daring to produce a book on painting, and, furthermore, on painting done in the 1970s, as it is for Patrick Heron to sound his clarion for those who relish and adore and idolise the art . . . But, of course, we know that art does not fit into neat decades and periods, that Pablo Picasso lived on long after Cubism and continued to make further contributions to the revolutions that followed, that Claude Monet continued to paint his lily-pads until 1926, and that they, along with Kasimir Malevich's red, black, and white squares or Pierre Bonnard's luscious peaches, look as fresh and immediately acceptable as they ever did, for contemporary art is such that it keeps alive the art of its own century; it is more a resurrectionist than grave-digger. Artists, like many in this book, span the decades; many practise painting not in defiance of other and newer modes, not as the only craft they know, but in a spirit of coexistence, however abrasive that may be.

Too little is written about how this century has expanded the uses of painting in art. Painting has had the most responsive reaction to the dynamic that has dominated this century: the force of the contemporary. If I read a title, ''What Happened to the Modern Novel?'', I am content to believe that a period of extreme experimentation in the novel has occurred, but should someone ask "Whatever Happened to Modern Painting?" I can only say that it is alive and well, because, with all the changes, switches, giddy succession of movements, and seemingly contrary impulses that this century has afforded, one acknowledges an inner dynamic and an inherent impetus that sends waves of modernism—wavelets and tidal monsters—ever breaking on our cultural shores. They often cast up signs of a life that we thought washed away and lost at sea. Indeed, our century, rather than succumbing to shipwreck each decade, has been so full of rescues or revivals that one needs to keep a dictionary of "Neo's" handy; Neo-dada, Neo-surrealism, Neo-art deco are with us; sometimes they deserve new nomenclature like Assemblage, Combine Painting, or Earth Art. If an eighteenth-century Englishman, his soul haunted by Gothic ghosts, builds a Gothic-turreted folly, why should not Robert Smithson build his folly, useless and haunting, as a spiral of earth and stones in Utah's salt lake?

All this is not to deny that there were stylistic characteristics of the 1960s (minimal art with bland, uninflected surfaces, linear, unpainterly, carefully ordered, and emotionally neutral) and of the 1950s (gestural vigour where line became mass and mass became a fluctuating area of overall energy), but what is surprising is that the decades overlap. For example, the forerunners of Pop Art were exhibiting in New York in 1955, in the heyday of the recognition of Action Painting; Ellsworth Kelly was a Minimalist long before the word was necessary; and, at the other end of the time scale, Adolph Gottlieb continued to refine, intensify, and elaborate his work into the 1970s. A quiet realist like Wayne Thiebaud was preparing the ground for a new realism of which we have a few suggestions in this book. All this could perhaps be put in a nutshell: since the first decade of this century artists and their admirers have not for one moment forgotten Henri Matisse.

We live in a century of both continuity and revivals. If our art, as Edward Lucie-Smith believes, has been living off the first two or three decades, it has done so by revivifying them, by being inspired by them in the purest sense. Such is the force of genuflection to the notion of the necessity of consciousness of an *avant garde* that any glance over one's shoulder at the geniuses who briefly touched down on this earth is considered a Bad Thing; such rear-visions, it is said, will lead to the evils of eclecticism. Eclecticism is often not chosen by but is thrust upon the artist. Who imagines that when in 1907 Pablo Picasso painted his largest painting to that date, *Les Demoiselles d'Avignon*, the most eclectic of masterpieces in this century, he went out with an eclectic shopping basket?

There is little polemical point in saying that Australian painting at present is influenced, often eclectic and sometimes, in its apprenticeship, following masters too closely. Those are the facts of life of art and artists. Who served as slavish an apprenticeship to Juan Miró and Pablo Picasso as Arshile Gorky before he established his independence and produced a generative art? Should this sound like defensive pleading, let it be said that there are in this book quite a number of painters of distinctive originality and quite a number who have so assimilated influences that their styles, approaches, and convictions are their own. Again, many have lived abroad; many have travelled widely, some live in the United States and Europe. Practising in the 1970s are some of the most experienced and informed painters in the history of Australian art. They are participants in rather than observers of certain aspects of international painting, but, in the main, they are Australian painters despite the wide variety of approaches—a variety, it might be added, that indicates conviction and not tentative experiments with this mode or that.

In almost all Australian painting of note there is still an urgency, a sense of frontal impact, a feeling of pressure and, at times, of anxiety. Even in our more decorative (no longer, one hopes, a dismissive adjective) artists there is a frisson of unease, even if it only suggests that the delightful world is transient. Even painters who admire the more delicate New York lyrical and geometric abstractionists achieve a note of quiet desperation in their canvases. Consequently Australian painting at present is not ruminative or contemplative; it is not low-keyed in emotion and hue as is much contemporary art abroad; it is not diagrammatic and coolly analytic; it is not an austere, intellectual exercise but is charged with feeling. As might be expected, it is, therefore, rather restless, fractured, intense in form and colour, and, even if artists might not think so, it is replete with symbols of the emotions. Except in a few cases form as the dominant icon has been shattered and dispersed across the canvas. In his lecture Patrick Heron recalled how he had advised a recomplication of the picture surface. Nowhere in the world does it swarm with incident, marks, comments, and a multitude of pictorial devices as in Australia. Nowhere is it so varied in approaches. Perhaps this is because artists, whose work can be seen more readily in Australian commercial galleries than work by their counterparts in New York City or London, are not driven in upon themselves and can evaluate their problems under the public gaze, a fact that ought to make the public more aware of its own participatory role.

Certainly the situation has led to a healthy tolerance (even if it is sometimes tainted by indifference) of various approaches. In turn, this coexistence, rivalry, and encounter of the different approaches, styles, and attitudes could be a launching pad for new and commanding painting. The constant presence of work by older, more experienced painters, who have continued to elaborate their themes and expand their means, alongside the work of younger painters who can still happily think their initial work is expendable, is culturally generative. It is not true that the past weighs like a mountain on the living; younger painters regard it as something to plunder, ignore, or cultivate; and so this book contains a number of established artists whose work has continued to develop into the 1970s and some whose work had just begun to achieve solidarity as the 1970s began. Some established artists, reproduction of whose work is readily available, have not been included, not because their work is no longer of influence, but because their production in the 1970s has not been significantly different. Naturally, there will be some disagreement with the choice of other artists, but a wide net has been cast. It could have been cast over some new Conceptualists, Anti-form, and Video artists, but the book was limited to painting.

No excuse is needed for that for it is a limitation and requirement that must only lead to re-echoing Patrick Heron's words and a reappraisal of the importance of the act of painting in Australian culture.

Elwyn Lynn

2 LOUIS JAMES
Reflected Images—1.50 approx. (1974)
183 x 152.5 cms
Oil on canvas
In the possession of the artist
Photograph: Stan Ciccone, Sydney 13

Left:
3 KEITH LOOBY
Stuffed & Split (1972)
167.5 x 167.5 cms
Acrylic on canvas
Collection: Mr & Mrs J. L. S. Girling, Canberra
Photograph: John Crowther, Canberra

Below:
4 RODNEY MILGATE
Thoughts on Holism (1974)
121.9 x 213.4 cms
Acrylic and oil on hardboard
Collection: Art Gallery of New South Wales, Sydney
Gift of Patrick White, 1974
Photograph: Stan Ciccone, Sydney

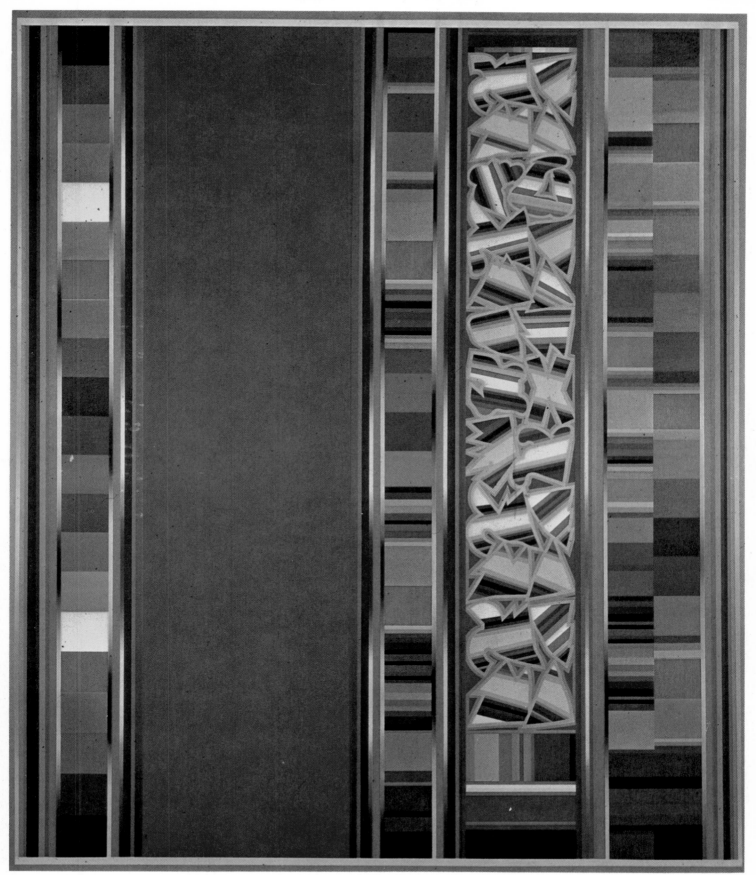

5 ALUN LEACH-JONES
Time and Silence II. Jacob's Ladder (1974)
243.8 x 203.2 cms
Acrylic on canvas
In the possession of the artist
Photograph: Dror Howley, Melbourne

Below:
6 JOHN COBURN
Enigma (1975)
91 x 91 cms
Acrylic on canvas
In the possession of the artist
Photograph: Stan Ciccone, Sydney

Facing Page Right:
7 JOHN HOWLEY
The Atomic Overlord (1972)
152.4 x 91.4 cms
Oil on canvas
In the possession of the artist
Photograph: Dror Howley, Melbourne

Below:
8 FRANZ KEMPF
Between Sea and Sky (1973–74)
122 x 122 cms
Oil on canvas
In the possession of the artist
Photograph: Colin Ballantyne & Partners, Adelaide

Below:
9 W. THOMAS ARTHUR
In Quest of "Not Know" (1974)
23.5 x 66 cms
Mixed media
Collection: "Thea Proctor Memorial Fund,"
Art Gallery of New South Wales, Sydney
Photograph: Kerry Dundas, Sydney

10 KEVIN CONNOR
Portrait of Ray Crooke (1974)
182.8 x 152.4 cms
Acrylic on canvas
In the possession of the artist
Photograph: John Delacour, Sydney

11 JAN SENBERGS
The Black Plank I (1972)
152.4 x 182.8 cms
Acrylic on canvas
Courtesy Rudy Komon Gallery, Sydney
Photograph: John Delacour, Sydney

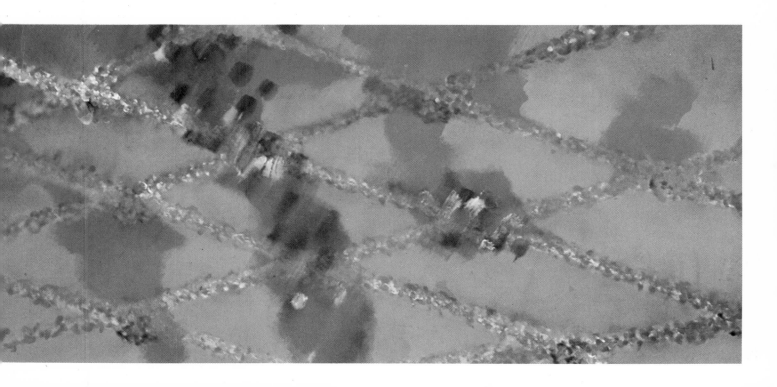

Left:
15 MARTIN SHARP
Birth of Venus (1973)
154 x 185 cms
Acrylic on canvas
Collection: Ian Fraser, Sydney
Photograph: Greg Weight, Sydney

Below:
16 GUY GREY-SMITH
Breakaway Country (1974)
91.4 x 121.9 cms
Oil on board
Collection: Mrs J. B. Gowing, Sydney
Photograph: Stan Ciccone, Sydney

Right:
18 BRIDGID McLEAN
Car Painting (1973)
152.4 x 121.9 cms
Acrylic on canvas
In the possession of the artist
Photograph: John Delacour, Sydney

Below:
17 BRIAN McKAY
Poros (1974)
122 x 132 cms
Oil on canvas
Collection: University of Western Australia
Photograph: Don Diamond, Perth

Right:
19 MICHAEL BROWN
Little Sheep (1972)
122 x 92 cms
Acrylic on hardboard
Private collection
Photograph: John Delacour, Sydney

20 COLIN LANCELEY
"The Object of all Travel is to Arrive at the Shores of the
Mediterranean"—Samuel Johnson (1970–71)
168 cms diameter
Oil on wood and canvas on circular stretcher
Collection: Mr & Mrs G. O'Neill, Sydney
Photograph: John Delacour, Sydney

21 JEFFREY MAKIN
Merton (1973)
184 x 245 cms
Oil on canvas
In the possession of the artist
Photograph: Stan Ciccone, Sydney

22 JOHN PEART
Grand Pink (1974)
231.7 x 431.1 cms
Acrylic on canvas
Collection: Philip Cox Storey & Partners, Sydney
Photograph: John Delacour, Sydney

23 JOHN FIRTH-SMITH
Wren's Favourite View (1975)
198 x 305 cms
Oil on canvas
Collection: Mr & Mrs G. Osborne, Sydney
Photograph: Robert Walker, Sydney

Right:
24 CLIFTON PUGH
Portrait of Don Dunstan (1972)
120 x 90 cms
Oil on board
Private collection
Photograph: John Delacour, Sydney

Right:
25 ERIC SMITH
The Painter Transmogrified and Mrs Smith (1973)
142.2 x 175.2 cms
Oil on canvas on hardboard
In the possession of the artist
Photograph: John Delacour, Sydney

Above:
26 DAVID ROSE
Bateau Bay (1973)
130 x 106 cms
Acrylic on canvas
Private collection
Photograph: Stan Ciccone, Sydney

Above:
27 ROYSTON HARPUR
Composition (1974)
42 x 47 cms
Ink on paper
Courtesy Hogarth Galleries, Sydney
Photograph: Douglas Thompson, Sydney

Right:
28 KEN REINHARD
To the Big E (1974)
94.5 x 155.5 cms
Acrylic, photocollage, chrome-plated brass
Collection: Ron Hodgson, Sydney
Photograph: Stan Ciccone, Sydney

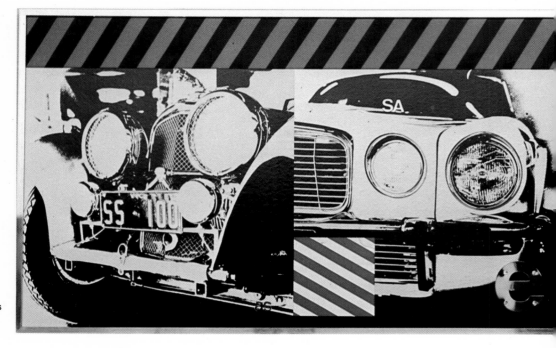

29 SIDNEY NOLAN
The Young Men Aspire like Departing Souls from Leaking Roofs—Ern Malley Series (1974)
152.4 x 122.9 cms
Oil on board
Private collection
Photographer unknown

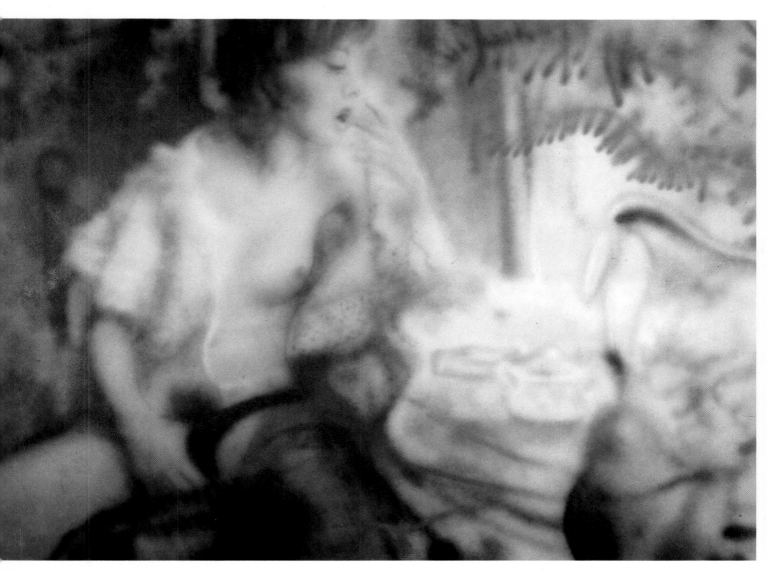

32 GEOFFREY PROUD
Untitled (1974)
167.6 x 227.3 cms
Oil on canvas
Collection: New South Wales Bar Association, Sydney
Photograph: John Delacour, Sydney

Right:
33 MARTIN COLLOCOTT
Blue III (1973)
213 x 366 cms
Acrylic on canvas
Collection: B.H.P. House, Melbourne
Photograph: Dror Howley, Melbourne

Below:
34 PETER UPWARD
Blue Note (1972)
182.9 x 121.9 cms
Acrylic on canvas
In the possession of the artist
Photograph: E. Sincic, Sydney

Below:
35 GEORGE HAYNES
XXX (1974)
168 x 140 cms
Acrylic on canvas
Private collection
Photograph: Richard Waldendorf, Perth

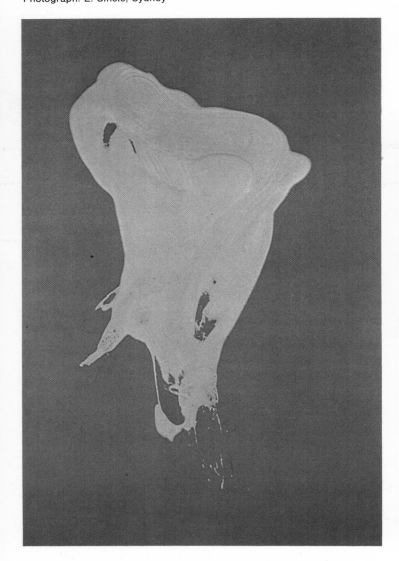

36 GUNTER CHRISTMANN
Chenden Gyaling (1970)
213.5 x 173 cms
Acrylic on canvas
Collection: Australian National Gallery, Canberra
Photograph: Douglas Thompson, Sydney

37 ROGER KEMP
Rhythmical Structure (1973)
168.9 x 228.6 cms
Acrylic on canvas
In the possession of the artist
Photograph: Dror Howley, Melbourne

Left:
38 RICHARD LARTER
That Special Disposition (1973)
180.3 x 114.3 cms
Acrylic on canvas
Collection: Mrs F. Welch, Adelaide
Photograph: J. B. Jensen, Adelaide

Below:
39 DONALD FRIEND
The Outrigger (1974)
56 x 75 cms
Gouache and acrylic on paper on board
Collection: Mark & Eva Besen, Melbourne
Photograph: Dror Howley, Melbourne

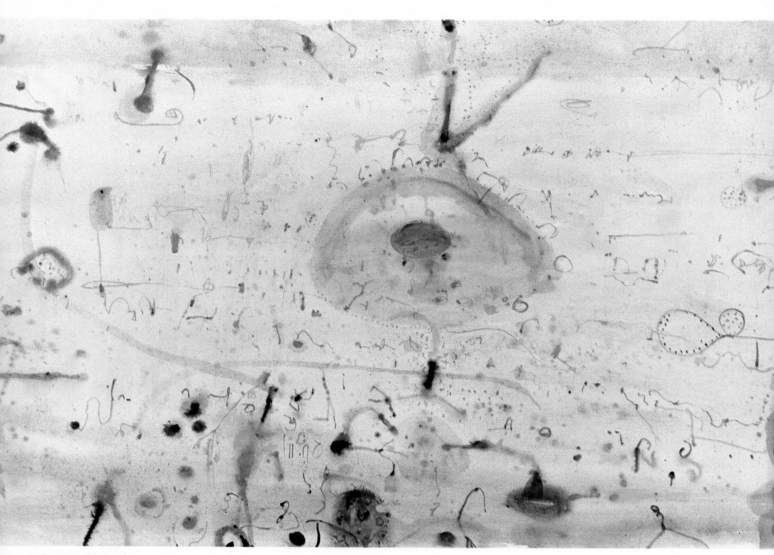

40 JOHN OLSEN
Frog Sounds (1975)
91.4 x 152.4 cms
Acrylic on paper
Courtesy Australian Galleries, Melbourne
Photograph: Val Foreman, Melbourne

Right:
41 ASHER BILU
Zone V (1974)
135 x 120 cms
Mixed media on plywood
In the possession of the artist
Photograph: Dror Howley, Melbourne

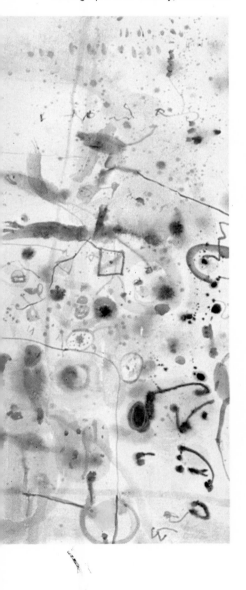

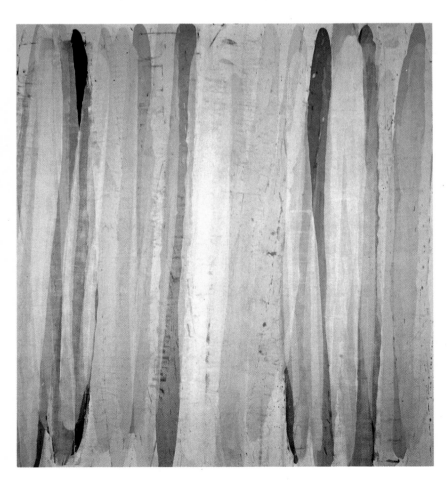

Right:
42 DAVID RANKIN
Black Duck Creek (1974)
176 x 160 cms
Acrylic on canvas
In the possession of the artist
Photograph: John Delacour, Sydney

Above:
43 PETER CLARKE
Orange on Grey (1974)
198 x 228 cms
Acrylic on canvas
In the possession of the artist
Photograph: Dror Howley, Melbourne

Above:
44 ANTON HOLZNER
Yesterday (1974)
182.8 x 152.4 cms
Oil on canvas
Collection: Mr & Mrs D. Tippett, Adelaide
Photograph: J. B. Jensen, Adelaide

Right:
45 ROBERT GRIEVE
Poissons d'Or—Homage to Debussy (1973)
121.9 x 152.4 cms
Acrylic on pineboard
In the possession of the artist
Photograph: Dror Howley, Melbourne

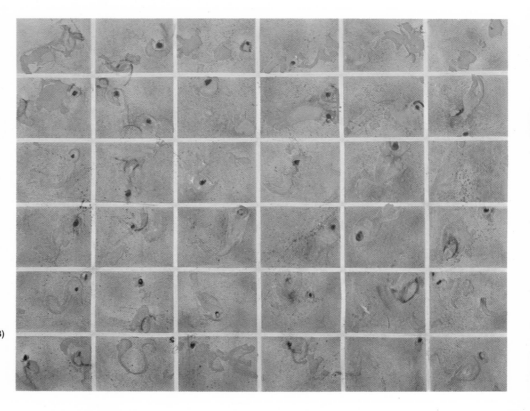

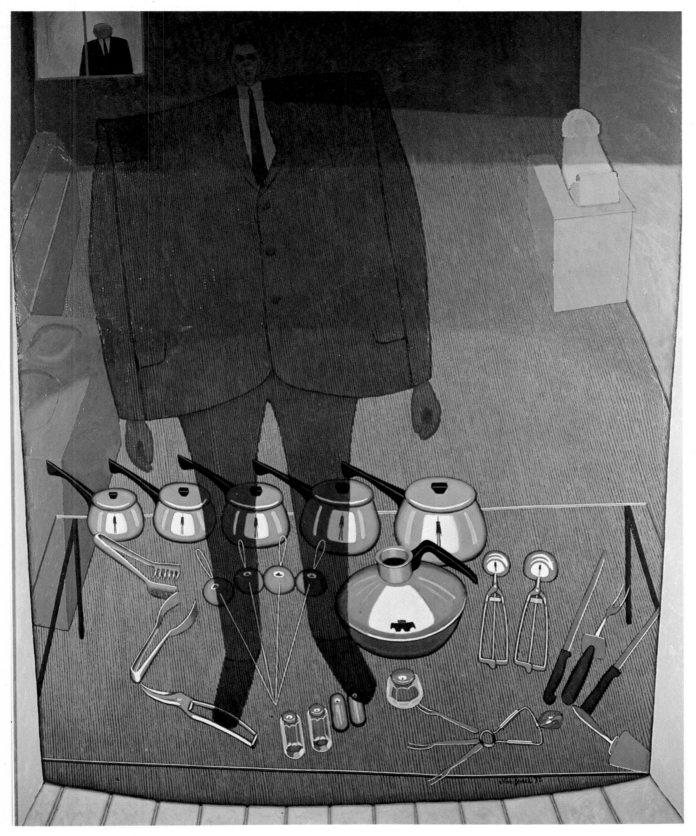

46 JOHN BRACK
Inside and Outside (The Shop Window) (1972)
164 x 130 cms
Oil on canvas
Collection: Australian National Gallery, Canberra
Photograph: Bill Baggett, Canberra

Left:
47 STEPHEN EARLE
The View from Up There (1973)
153.4 x 153.4 cms
Acrylic on canvas
In the possession of the artist
Photograph: Stan Ciccone, Sydney

Right:
48 LAWRENCE DAWS
The 1913 Mining Disaster (1970)
121.9 x 121.9 cms
Oil on canvas
Courtesy Rudy Komon Gallery, Sydney
Photograph: Stan Ciccone, Sydney

49 WILLIAM DELAFIELD COOK
Leaves (1973)
152.4 x 152.4 cms
Acrylic on canvas
Collection: Elton John, England
Photograph: Rodney Todd-White, London

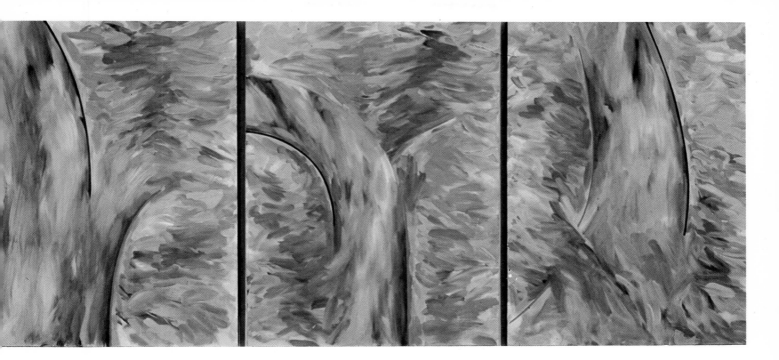

Above:
53 JANET DAWSON
Balgalal Creek Gums (1974)
121.9 x 274.3 cms
Acrylic on linen
Collection: Mr & Mrs J. Lewis, Sydney
Photograph: Stan Ciccone, Sydney

Left:
54 ROBIN WALLACE-CRABBE
Principles of Duality (1973)
166 x 117 cms
Acrylic on canvas
Collection: Mr & Mrs David Chapman, Melbourne
Photograph: Dror Howley, Melbourne

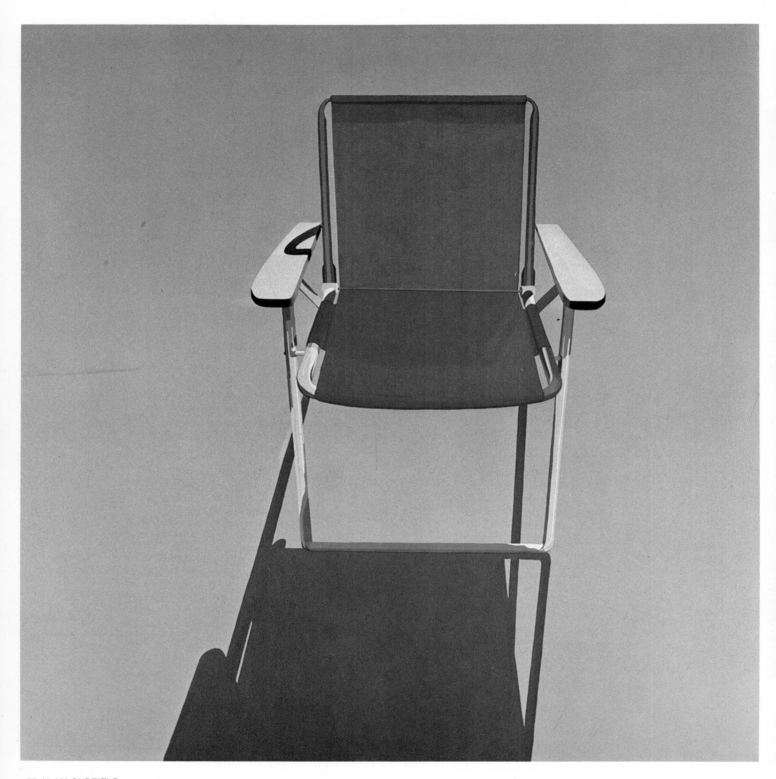

55 ALAN OLDFIELD
Red Chair (1972)
121.9 x 121.9 cms
Acrylic on canvas
Collection: The Philip Morris Arts Grant, Melbourne
Photograph: Dror Howley, Melbourne

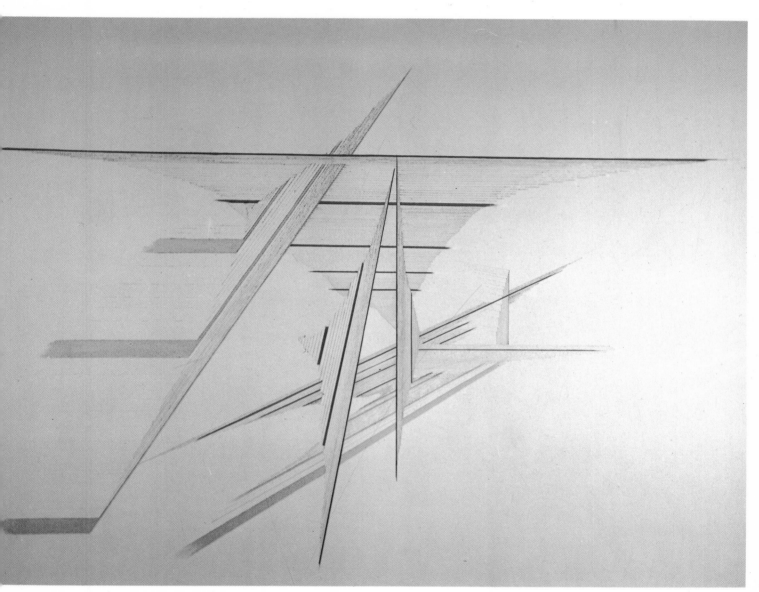

56 FRANZ LA GRANGE
Dynamic Harmony (1973)
216 x 154 cms
Acrylic on canvas
Courtesy Hogarth Galleries, Sydney
Photograph: David Liddle, Sydney

62 DAVID ASPDEN
Early One Morning (1974)
121.9 x 274.3 cms
Acrylic on cotton duck
Courtesy Rudy Komon Gallery, Sydney
Photograph: John Delacour, Sydney

63 PETER TYNDALL
Untitled Painting No. 17 (1974–75)
55.8 x 40.6 cms
Oil on canvas
In the possession of the artist
Photograph: Adrian Featherston, Melbourne

Right:
64 NEVIL MATTHEWS
Through (1972)
119 x 194 cms
Polyester dyes on shaped particle board
In the possession of the artist
Photograph: Stan Ciccone, Sydney

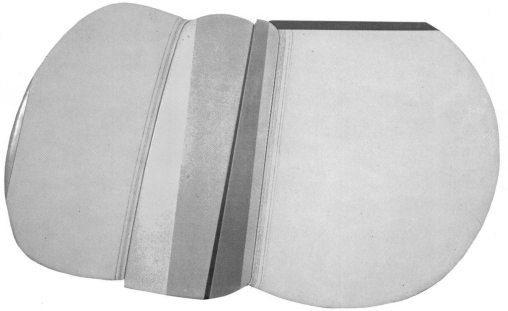

Right:
65 W. (BILL) BROWN
Get Back (1972)
248 x 179 cms
Acrylic on canvas
Courtesy Bonython Gallery, Sydney
Photograph: John Delacour, Sydney

Below:
66 CHARLES BLACKMAN
Girl Listening to Music (1972)
137.1 x 243.8 cms
Oil on hardboard
Gift of Mr Akio Morita, President
of Sony Corporation of Japan, by kind
permission of Sydney Opera House Trust
Photograph: John Delacour, Sydney

Below:
67 LEONARD FRENCH
River of Stars (1973)
182.8 x 152.4 cms
Enamel on hessian-covered hardboard
In the possession of the artist
Photograph: Stan Ciccone, Sydney

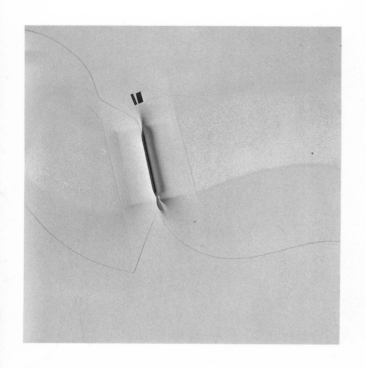

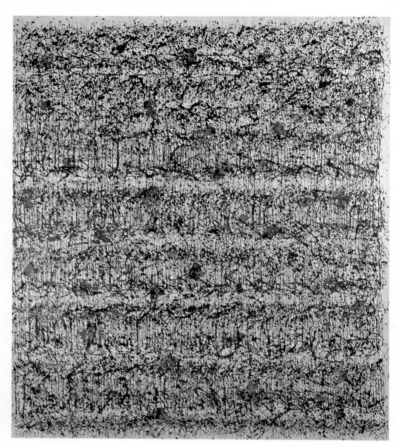

Above:
68 BELA IVANYI
Yellow Rhythm (1974)
168 x 172 cms
Acrylic on canvas
Courtesy Hogarth Galleries, Sydney
Photograph: Stan Ciccone, Sydney

Facing Page Left:
69 JOSEPH SZABO
Untitled (1972)
211.4 x 186.3 cms
Synthetic polymer paint on cotton duck
Collection: Art Gallery of New South Wales, Sydney
Gift of Patrick White, 1972
Photograph: Kerry Dundas, Sydney

Above:
71 MICHAEL JOHNSON
Veronese (1974)
243.8 x 283.8 cms
Flash vinylic colour on canvas
In the possession of the artist
Photograph: Stan Ciccone, Sydney

Facing Page, Bottom:
70 DICK WATKINS
Untitled (1970)
169.5 x 186.6 cms
Acrylic on canvas
Collection: Art Gallery of New South Wales, Sydney.
Gift of Patrick White
Photograph: Kerry Dundas, Sydney

72 BRETT WHITELEY
Big Orange (Sunset) (1974)
244 x 305 cms
Oil on plywood
Collection: Art Gallery of New South Wales, Sydney
Gift of Patrick White, 1975
Photograph: Stan Ciccone, Sydney

Left:
73 TERENCE O'DONNELL
Kookaburra (1972)
167.6 x 198.1 cms
Acrylic on canvas
Collection: David Chesney, Sydney
Photograph: Stan Ciccone, Sydney

Left:
74 LLOYD REES
Moving Waters (1974)
60.9 x 73.6 cms
Oil on canvas, mounted on hardboard
In the possession of the artist
Photograph: Stan Ciccone, Sydney

Left:
75 MIRIAM STANNAGE
Shadows on a Grey Window (1972)
147.3 x 147.3 cms
Acrylic on canvas
Courtesy Hogarth Galleries, Sydney
Photograph: Stan Ciccone, Sydney

Right:
76 ROBERT OWEN
Grey Day (1974)
121.9 x 121.9 cms
Perspex, graphite and wax on wood
In the possession of the artist
Photograph: Stan Ciccone, Sydney

Left:
77 CHRISTOPHER WALLIS
Wyargine (1975)
127 x 177.8 cms
Acrylic on canvas
In the possession of the artist
Photograph: Stan Ciccone, Sydney

78 ARTHUR BOYD
Kneeling Figure with Canvas and Black Can (1973)
114.3 x 190.2 cms
Oil on canvas
Collection: Australian National Gallery, Canberra
Photographer unknown

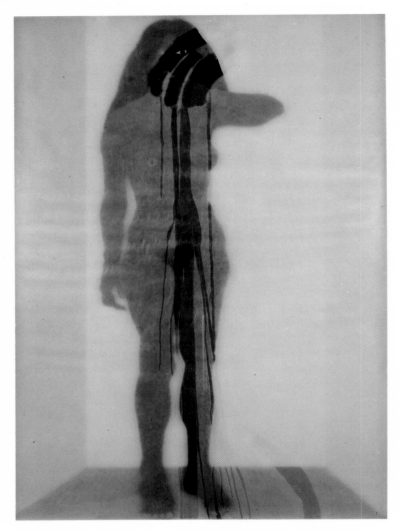

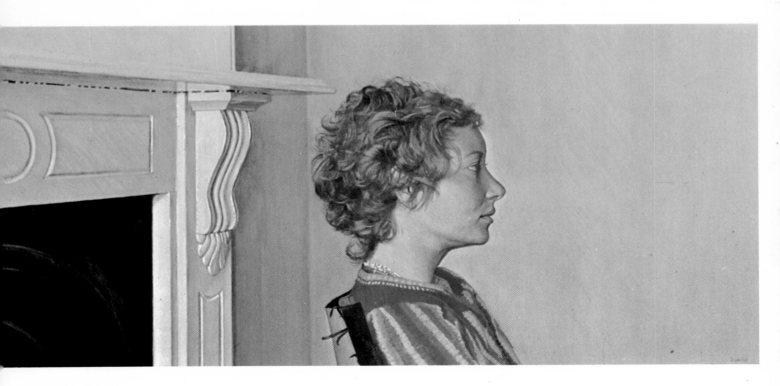

81 BRYAN WESTWOOD
Storm Going Away, Centennial Park (1975)
122 x 122 cms
Oil on board
Courtesy Bonython Gallery, Sydney
Photograph: John Delacour, Sydney

Below:
82 IVAN DURRANT
Man about Town (1972)
103 x 120 cms
Acrylic on board
In the possession of the artist
Photograph: Dror Howley, Melbourne

Below:
84 GUY WARREN
Untitled (1973)
157.4 x 279.3 cms
Acrylic on canvas
Collection: Western Australian Art Gallery
Photograph: Stan Ciccone, Sydney

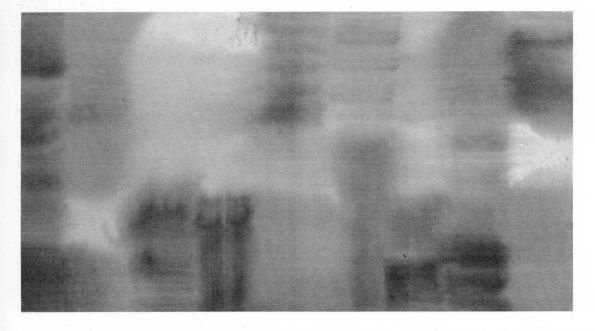

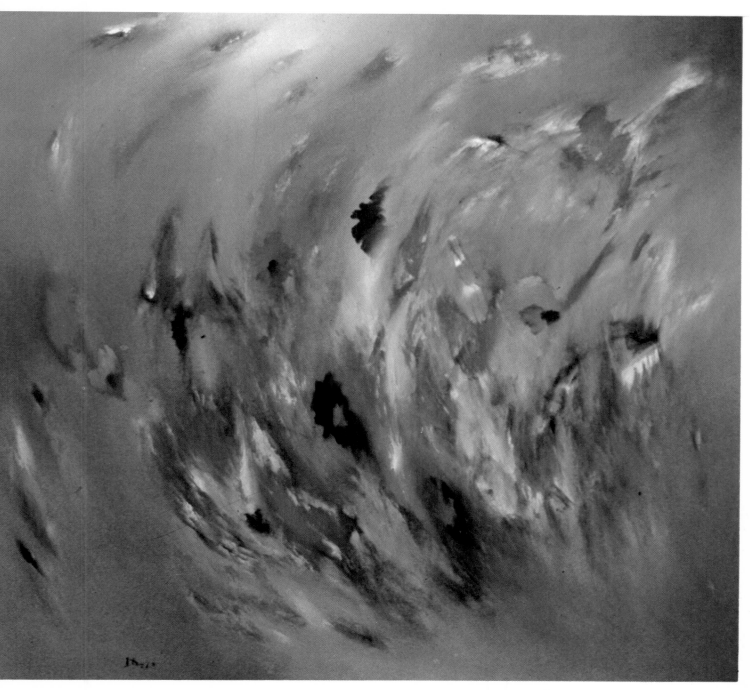

Right:
86 GARETH SANSOM
Untitled (1975)
177.8 x 203.2 cms
Enamel on linen canvas
In the possession of the artist
Photograph: John Bolton, Melbourne

Below:
87 RON ROBERTSON-SWANN
On the Wings of an Eagle (1972)
90.1 x 173.9 cms
Acrylic on duck
Collection: Abbey Orchard, Sydney
Photograph: John Delacour, Sydney

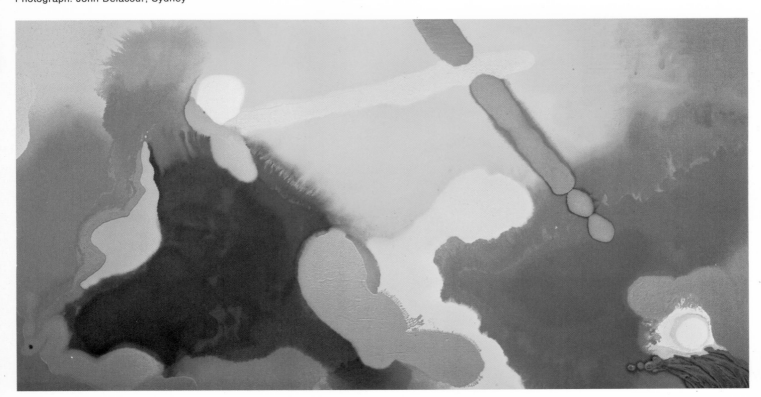

88 RAY CROOKE
Village at Yalombi, Fiji (1974)
121.9 x 91.4 cms
Oil and acrylic on canvas, mounted on hardboard
Private collection
Photograph: Tim Collis-Bird, Sydney

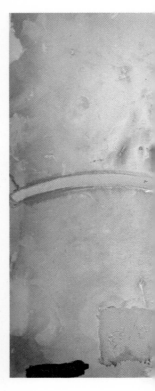

89 FRED WILLIAMS
Forest (1974)
106.6 x 91.4 cms
Oil on canvas
In the possession of the artist
Photograph: Dror Howley, Melbourne

90 FRED CRESS
Bokhara (1973)
152.4 x 365.7 cms
Acrylic on canvas
Collection: Dr & Mrs D. Rosenthal, Melbourne
Photograph: Dror Howley, Melbourne

Above:
91 VIRGINIA JAY
Disjoin II (1974)
213 x 305 cms
Acrylic on canvas
Collection: Robert Ashton, Sydney
Photograph: Stan Ciccone, Sydney

Below
92 ROBERT JACKS
Knave Paltry and Poghuing Picked Green (1972)
91 x 91 cms
Oil on canvas
Collection: Art Gallery of New South Wales, Sydney
Photograph: Kerry Dundas, Sydney

Left:
93 GIL JAMIESON
Kangaroo Skinners (1974)
121.9 x 132 cms
Oil on canvas
In the possession of the artist
Photograph: Stan Ciccone, Sydney

94 ALBERT TUCKER
Melbourne, Night (1974)
56 x 72 cms
Acrylic on board
In the possession of the artist
Photograph: Dror Howley, Melbourne

Right:
95 COL JORDAN
Whole (1973)
173 x 137 cms
Acrylic on canvas
Courtesy Bonython Gallery, Sydney
Photograph: Stan Ciccone, Sydney

Below:
96 ALLAN MITELMAN
Wolverine 2 (1974)
55.8 x 73.6 cms
Mixed media on paper
Collection: Robert Brunton, Melbourne
Photograph: John Bolton, Melbourne

97 TIM STORRIER
Morning on the Oranoko (1974)
152.5 x 244 cms
Acrylic on canvas
Collection: David McMahon, Sydney
Photograph: Stan Ciccone, Sydney

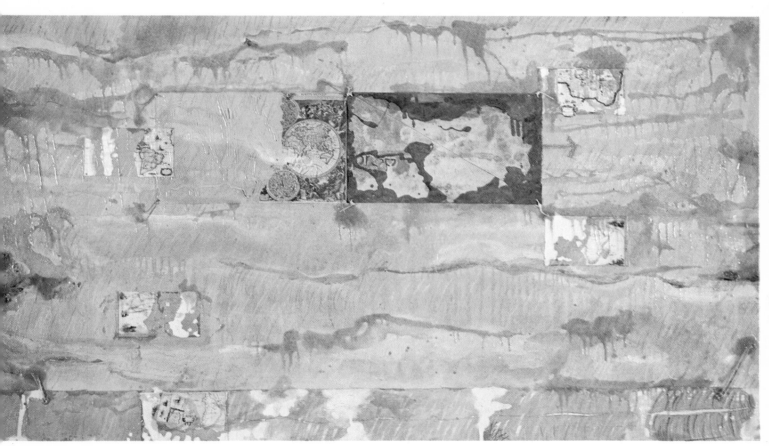

103 LES KOSSATZ
Abacas 2—Rabbit Series (1973–74)
170.1 x 170.1 cms
Oil on canvas
Private collection
Photograph: John Edson, Melbourne

74

106 JEFFREY SMART
Truck and Trailer Approaching a City (1974)
75 x 150 cms
Acrylic on canvas
Courtesy Rudy Komon Gallery, Sydney
Photograph: Stan Ciccone, Sydney

107 ROBERT JUNIPER
Evening Rider (1974)
170 x 180 cms
Acrylic and oil on canvas
Private collection
Photograph: Richard Waldendorf, Perth

Below:
109 VYTAS SERELIS
Me (1972)
92 x 132 cms
Oil on acrylic on canvas
Collection: Loene Serelis, Adelaide
Photograph: Grant Matthews, Adelaide

Above:
108 FRANK HODGKINSON
Anastomosis (1972)
182.9 x 152.4 cms
Acrylic on canvas
In the possession of the artist
Photograph: Stan Ciccone, Sydney

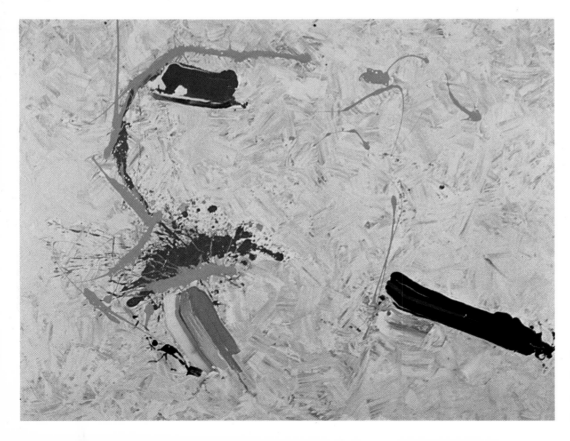

Left:
110 ROSS JACKSON
Island Series 5—Jubilant I (1974)
164 x 208 cms
Acrylic on cotton duck
In the possession of the artist
Photograph: Stan Ciccone, Sydney

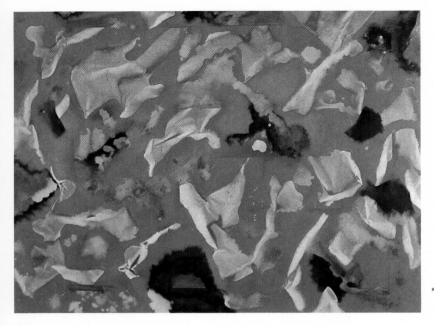

Left:
111 RICHARD HAVYATT
Turning the Circuit (1973)
157.4 x 205.7 cms
Acrylic on canvas
In the possession of the artist
Photograph: Dror Howley, Melbourne

Right:
112 KEN WHISSON
Pub Conversation (1972)
81.2 x 104.1 cms
Oil on board
Private collection
Photograph: Stan Ciccone, Sydney

Left:
113 SHAY DOCKING
South Seas Icon No. 11—Horn of the Earth (1972)
165 x 214 cms
Oil tempera and acrylic on hardboard
Collection: Art Gallery of New South Wales, Sydney
Photograph: Les Lloyd, Dunedin

114 ROBERT BOYNES
Strike (1974)
152.4 x 152.4 cms
Acrylic on canvas
In the possession of the artist
Photograph: J. B. Jensen, Adelaide

Biographical Notes and Index

ARTHUR, THOMAS. (9) Born 1946, Massachusetts. Graduate studies at Boston Museum of Fine Arts and Tufts University, Mass. Recipient of six U.S. awards. Participated in group shows in U.S.A. and Australia. One-man show 1974. Represented in the Art Gallery of N.S.W.

ASPDEN, DAVID. (62) Born 1935, England. Came to Australia in 1950. Travelled to France and England 1971–72. Eleven one-man shows in Sydney and Melbourne; participated in Sao Paulo Bienal 1971, Sydney Biennale 1973. Represented in several State galleries and many private collections.

BALDESSIN, GEORGE. (12) Born 1939, Melbourne. Studied at Royal Melbourne Institute of Technology, 1958–61, and Academy of Fine Arts of the Brera Museum, Milan, under the sculptor Marino Marini, 1962–63. Visited Japan in 1966 and South America where he represented Australia in the Sao Paulo Bienal 1975. He has won noted prizes such as the Alcorso Sekers Prize for Sculpture, Comalco Prize for Sculpture, and second drawing prize at the 1970 Biennale for Drawing, Yugoslavia. He has had five one-man shows since 1964, and has participated in important painting and print shows sent abroad. Represented in the National Gallery, Canberra; several State and regional galleries; and in many private collections.

BALL, SYDNEY. (1) Born 1933, Adelaide. Studied South Australian School of Art and Art Students League, N.Y.C. Lived in New York City for two periods in 1960s and 1970s. Has had fourteen one-man shows and participated in many group shows, including Sydney Biennale and "Ten Australians." Represented in all State galleries; National Gallery; regional, university, and private collections; museums in U.S.A., Yugoslavia, and Thailand.

BILU, ASHER. (41) Born 1936, Tel Aviv. Came to Australia 1957. Ten one-man shows after first in Melbourne, 1960, in Australia, Holland, and England. Won Blake and H. C. Richards prizes 1965. Represented in the National Gallery, Canberra; National Gallery of Victoria; Contemporary Art Society, London; and in private collections in Australia and abroad.

BLACKMAN, CHARLES. (66) Born 1928, Sydney. Studied art privately; press-artist, Sydney *Sun*. Has lived in Melbourne (member of the Antipodeans), Sydney, Brisbane, London, and Paris. Among other awards and prizes, he won the Helena Rubinstein Scholarship. Has had twenty one-man shows in all Australian capitals and abroad. Represented in the National Gallery, Canberra; all State galleries; regional, university, and private collections (in Australia and abroad); Worcester Museum, U.S.A.; and Musée d'Art Moderne, Paris.

BOOTH, PETER. (83) Born 1940, Sheffield, England. Studied Sheffield College of Art and National Gallery School, Melbourne, after arrival in Australia in 1958. One-man shows in Melbourne and Sydney since 1969. Represented in "Recent Australian Art" Art Gallery of N.S.W. 1973.

BOYD, ARTHUR. (78) Born 1920, Melbourne. Studied with grandfather, Arthur Merric Boyd, National Gallery School, Melbourne. Travelled to London 1959; returned to live in Australia 1975. Some forty one-man shows in England and Australia, the first in 1937 in Melbourne, with retrospectives at the Whitechapel Gallery, London in 1962, South Australian Art Gallery 1964, and in Edinburgh 1969. Widely represented in galleries in Australia and in private collections in Australia and England. Franz Philipp's book on the artist and the Komon Gallery's on his drawings are important.

BOYNES, ROBERT. (114) Born 1942, Adelaide. Studied at South Australian School of Art. Worked and studied in England for two years after he left Australia in 1967; lives in Adelaide. He has had one-man shows in Adelaide, Sydney, Melbourne, and London and has participated in invitational group shows abroad. He has won several prizes of note, including the 1971 Barossa Arts Festival award. Represented in the National Gallery, Canberra; several State and regional collections; and privately.

BRACK, JOHN. (46) Born 1920, Melbourne. Studied National Gallery School, Melbourne, 1946–49. Head of that school, 1962–68. First one-man show in 1953 and many followed in Sydney, Melbourne, Brisbane, and Adelaide. Won the Travelodge Art Prize 1971. Represented in all State galleries; National Gallery, Canberra; regional galleries; and widely in private collections.

BRISCOE, KATE. (50) Born 1944, Corby, Northamptonshire. Gained Teacher's Diploma, Leicester College of Art 1964–65. Taught, designed costumes, exhibited in England 1965–68. Travelled through Europe, the Middle East, and India to Australia in 1969. Since 1968 she has had five one-woman shows in England and Sydney; has participated in a number of print and painting group shows abroad and in Australia, such as the World Print Competition, San Francisco 1973. In 1975 she won the Cathay Pacific Art Prize. Represented in private collections in England and Australia.

BROWN, MICHAEL. (19) Born 1938, Sydney. Studied National Art School, Sydney. Came to notice in 1962 with Ross Crothall and Colin Lanceley with satirical, dadaist exhibitions, "Annandale Imitation Realists" (Museum of Modern Art, Melbourne), and "Subterranean Imitation Realists" (Rudy Komon Gallery, Sydney). Seven one-man shows since 1963. Represented in the Art Gallery of N.S.W.; Art Gallery of South Australia; and in private collections.

BROWN, WILLIAM (BILL). (65) Born 1945, Cowra, N.S.W. Studied at National Art School, Newcastle. Art teacher 1969–75. Visited Europe 1975. One-man shows in Sydney and Melbourne. Represented in the Art Gallery of N.S.W. and the National Gallery, Canberra.

CASSAB, JUDY. (30) Hungarian, born Vienna. Studied in Budapest and Prague. Has had twenty one-woman shows throughout Australia and two in London. Has won the Archibald Prize twice, the Helena Rubinstein Prize (Perth) twice, and the Sir Charles Lloyd Jones Memorial Prize on four occasions. C.B.E. 1969. Widely known as a portrait painter, but equally versed in abstraction. Represented in the State galleries of N.S.W., South Australia, Queensland, and Western Australia; National Gallery, Canberra; National Portrait Gallery, London; National Gallery, Budapest.

CHRISTMANN, GUNTER. (36) Born 1936, Berlin. Travelled to Canada 1956 and to Australia 1959. Part-time studies at National Art School, Sydney, but considers himself self-taught. Since 1968 has had fourteen one-man shows in Sydney, Melbourne, Perth, Canberra, Berlin, and Lubeck, the last two while on a scholarship in Germany 1973–74. Represented in Sao Paulo Bienal 1971, Sydney Biennale 1973, and permanently in Art Gallery of N.S.W.; National Gallery of Victoria; Western Australian Art Gallery; and National Gallery, Canberra.

CLARKE, PETER. (43) Born 1935, Deloraine, Tasmania. Studied Prahran Technical College and Royal Melbourne Technical College. Toured Europe 1961–62 and Europe and U.S.A. 1974. Has had twelve one-man shows in Melbourne, Sydney, and Brisbane since 1957. Represented in the National Gallery, Canberra; Art Gallery of N.S.W.; Newcastle City Gallery; and Melbourne and Queensland universities. Has won, among others, the H. C. Richards and Crouch prizes.

COBURN, JOHN. (6) Born Ingham, Queensland. Studied at East Sydney Technical College where he taught 1959–66 and became Head, 1972–74. Lived in Paris 1969–72 where he designed the Aubusson tapestries for the Sydney Opera House. Has had eighteen one-man shows since 1957. Represented in all State galleries; National Gallery, Canberra; regional galleries; the Vatican Museum, Rome; and the John F. Kennedy Center, Washington.

COLLOCOTT, MARTIN. (33) Born 1945, Sydney. Studied at the National Art School, East Sydney 1960–65. Since 1967 he has had ten one-man shows in London, Melbourne, Sydney, and Canberra. He has been included in notable mixed exhibitions in Australia, London, and U.S.A. In 1968 he lived in London and in 1972 won the International Telephone and Telegraph award. Represented in the National Gallery, Canberra; I.T. and T., New York City; and in private collections in Australia and overseas.

CONNOR, KEVIN. (10) Born 1932, Sydney. Studied night art school and Joss Holloway's Sketch Club, 1951. In 1952–56 he worked his way round the world; he painted in England, Canada, and U.S.A. Again to Europe in 1965, to U.S.A. on a Harkness Fellowship 1966. Painted in New York City, 1967–68. Twenty-five one-man shows in Australia and London. Represented in Sydney Biennale 1973 and in most State galleries; National Gallery, Canberra; universities; and private collections.

COUNIHAN, NOEL. (31) Born 1913, Melbourne. Self-taught painter and print-maker. First one-man show in Melbourne 1933; since then has had many one-man shows in Europe (where he lived 1949–52 and 1973–74) and Australia. Retrospective, National Gallery of Victoria and the Commonwealth Institute, London 1973. Represented in all State galleries; National Gallery, Canberra; regional, university, and private collections; and Toronto Art Gallery.

CRESS, FRED. (90) Born 1938, Poona, India. Lived in England 1948–61. Came to Australia 1962, toured Europe, U.S.A. 1966. Since 1965 has had twelve one-man shows in Melbourne, Sydney, and Brisbane. Included in "Ten Australians" touring show, 1975. Represented in the Western Australian Art Gallery; Melbourne University; Bendigo Teachers' College.

CROOKE, RAY. (88) Born 1922, Auburn, Victoria. Studied at Swinburne Technical College before and after the second World War when he became familiar with northern Queensland. Since 1949 has had many one-man shows: war studies, Queensland, New Guinea, and Fiji; retrospective, 1972 Adelaide Festival and first show in London, 1974. Represented in the National Gallery, Canberra; all State galleries; and many regional collections.

CUPPAIDGE, VIRGINIA. (52) Born 1943, Brisbane. Studied at Orban Art School 1960–62 and with John Olsen and Robert Kippel 1963. First one-woman show in 1961. Went to New York City 1969, where she had a one-woman show in 1973. Represented in the National Gallery, Canberra; Chase Manhattan Bank, N.Y.C.; and in private collections in U.S.A. and Australia.

DAWS, LAWRENCE. (48) Born 1927, Adelaide. Studied architecture and engineering then art at Melbourne National Gallery School. Worked in Rome and London for ten years and returned to Australia in 1970. Travels annually to London for print-making and now lives in Queensland. Has held twenty-one shows since 1950 throughout Australia and in Rome, London, and Oxford. Represented in the National Gallery, Canberra; all State galleries and all universities; also Scottish National Gallery of Modern Art; and the Victoria and Albert Museum, London.

DAWSON, JANET. (53) Born 1935, Sydney. Studied National Gallery Art School, Melbourne; Slade School, London; and in Paris and London. One-woman shows in Melbourne, Sydney, and Adelaide since 1961. Master printer for a number of artists, theatre set and poster designer, she has also planned museum installations. Represented in the National Gallery, Canberra; National Gallery of Victoria; Art Gallery of N.S.W.; Stedelijk Museum, Amsterdam; and with graphics in all State galleries.

DELAFIELD COOK, WILLIAM. (49) Born 1936, Melbourne. Studied Caulfield Technical College, Royal Melbourne College of Technology, University of Melbourne Bath Academy, and later, British School, Rome. One-man shows in Melbourne, London, and Berlin date from 1967; between 1956 and 1963 he was included in group shows in London, Melbourne, and Frankfurt and in "Revitalising Realism," 1972, in Eindhoven (Holland) and Brussels. He won the Georges Prize in 1971 and was awarded a German scholarship 1973–74. Represented in the National Gallery, Canberra; Art Gallery of South Australia; and National Gallery of Victoria.

DE TELIGA, STAN. (60) Born 1924, Poland. Came to Australia 1926 and studied at National Art School, Sydney. He has been Keeper at the Tasmanian Art Gallery and Director of the Blaxland Gallery,

Sydney. Since 1958 he has had fourteen one-man shows, gained the Flotta Lauro Scholarship 1968, and a British Council Grant 1970. Represented in the National Gallery, Canberra; State galleries of N.S.W., Tasmania, and South Australia.

DOCKING, SHAY. (113) Born 1928, Warrnambool, Victoria. Studied at Swinburne Technical College and National Gallery School, Melbourne. Lived in New Zealand for seven years from 1965 and was fascinated by volcanic geological forms. Since 1961 she has had twenty-one one-woman shows throughout Australia and New Zealand. Represented in group shows in Japan, U.S.A., Europe, and the Pacific; and in the collections of the National Gallery, Canberra; State galleries of N.S.W., Victoria, Western Australia, and South Australia; and six public galleries in New Zealand.

DUNLOP, BRIAN. (80) Born 1938, Sydney. Studied at the National Art School, Sydney. Travelled in Europe 1960. 1963–68 lived in Europe and Morocco. Has had eleven one-man shows in Sydney, Adelaide, and Canberra since 1962. Represented in the Art Gallery of N.S.W.; Art Gallery of South Australia; and in private collections in Australia, Europe, and U.S.A.

DURRANT, IVAN. (82) Born 1947, Melbourne. Graduated in Economics, Monash University. Since 1970 he has had seven one-man shows in Melbourne and Sydney. In 1975 he became involved in two widely discussed "Public Art Happenings"—a fake amputation of a hand and the display of a slaughtered cow—in order to make people more aware of what slaughter means and to create an audience for a concept. He is well represented in a number of private collections.

EARLE, STEPHEN. (47) Born 1942, Sydney. Studied at the National Art School, Sydney. Since 1947 has had eight one-man shows in Sydney and Adelaide. He has won a number of prizes including the Corio, 1970, and the Muswellbrook Prize, 1971. Represented in the National Gallery, Canberra; Art Gallery of N.S.W.; Art Gallery of South Australia; and public galleries of Newcastle and Launceston.

ELENBERG, JOEL. (58) Born 1948, Melbourne. Mainly self-taught except for a brief period spent at National Gallery Art School, Melbourne. At seventeen travelled through Middle East and Greece, returning to Australia from Israel in 1968. He has exhibited regularly since 1969 in Australia, most exhibitions including sculpture as well as paintings. In 1974 he worked with the Australian Broadcasting Commission's Natural History unit in Western Australia.

FIRTH-SMITH, JOHN. (23) Born 1943, Melbourne; lived in New Zealand 1945–52. Studied at the National Art School, Sydney. Since 1966 has had six one-man shows in Sydney and Melbourne. Worked in New York City 1971 and visited Europe in 1971 and 1973. Represented in Young Painters' Biennale, Paris, 1971; "Ten Australians" (tour of Europe), 1975; Sydney Biennale, 1973; and in State collections of N.S.W., Western Australia, and South Australia; Power Gallery of Contemporary Art; National Gallery, Canberra; and various regional galleries.

FRENCH, LEONARD. (67) Born 1928, Melbourne. Studied at the Royal Melbourne Technical College and abroad. Has won many prizes and is a distinguished muralist and designer of stained glass installations. Since 1949 he has had eighteen one-man shows throughout Australia and in London. Lived in U.S.A. in 1964 when he gained a Harkness Fellowship taken at Yale University. In 1969 he received the O.B.E. and in 1972 an Honorary Doctorate at Monash University. He has been represented in important exhibitions abroad, including the Sao Paulo Bienal, 1963. Represented in the National Gallery, Canberra; all State, many regional, and university collections; also in Museum of Modern Art, New York City.

FRIEND, DONALD. (39) Born 1915, Sydney. Studied at Westminster School, London. Official war artist in second World War. At various times he has lived in Nigeria, Torres Strait Islands, Hill End, Florence, Ceylon, Greece, and Bali where he now lives. As well as holding many one-man shows throughout Australia, he has written five books. In his sixtieth year he had a retrospective at the Holdsworth Gallery, 1975. Represented in National Collection, Canberra; all State galleries; many regional galleries; and extensively in private collections.

FULLBROOK, SAM. (61) Born 1922, Sydney. Studied at National Gallery School, Melbourne. Has exhibited in all capital cities and is represented in the National Gallery, Canberra, and all State collections. He won the Wynne Prize in 1961, shared that prize with David Strachan in 1963, and won the Archibald Prize in 1974. Much of his work derives from his interest in the Aborigines and their country.

GORDON, JEREMY. (104) Born 1947, Adelaide. Studied at the South Australian School of Art and East Sydney Technical College; he was privately tutored by the late Sir William Dobell. He returned to Australia in 1969 after travelling throughout Europe. He has exhibited in Sydney, Melbourne, and Adelaide since 1971 and is represented in the Reserve Bank of Australia and Flinders University.

GREY-SMITH, GUY. (16) Born 1916, Western Australia. Studied at Chelsea School of Art, London, 1945–47, fresco-painting at Central School, London, 1952–54, and pottery at Woolwich. His first one-man show was in Perth, 1949 and he has since been in Sydney, Melbourne, Brisbane, and Adelaide. In 1973 he received a special award from the Australia Council as a "distinguished artist." Represented in all State galleries and Leicester County Authority.

GRIEVE, ROBERT. (45) Born 1924, Melbourne. Studied in London and Japan, making study trips to Japan in 1962, 1964, and 1970. He is interested in signs, symbols, ideographs, script, calligraphy, and collage. Represented in most State galleries and in the National Gallery, Canberra; the Waikato Art Museum; and in private collections in Japan, U.S.A., and Australia.

HARPUR, ROYSTON. (27) Born 1938, Sydney. Studied with Maximilian Feuerring. Lived in London and Malta 1965; Gallery Manager, Institute of Contemporary Art, London 1965; Central Street Gallery 1966. He has worked with the National Gallery of Victoria and in 1972 lived and worked in Japan, studying Sumi-e with Shotei Ibata. He has been art critic on several journals. Since 1961 he has had twelve one-man shows in Sydney, Adelaide, Melbourne, Kyoto, Newcastle, and Maitland. He has participated in noted group shows in Australia and abroad and has won ten prizes since 1967. Represented in the Art Gallery of New South Wales; University of Sydney; Museum of Modern Art, Yugoslavia; and in city and private collections.

HAVYATT, RICHARD. (111) Born 1945, Melbourne. Studied Architecture at Melbourne University 1962–64. Began exhibiting in 1964 and had his first one-man show in 1967. He has exhibited in Sydney, Melbourne, and Ballarat. Twice winner, in 1968 and 1969, of the Minnie Crouch Prize for Watercolours. Represented in the National Gallery, Canberra; the National Gallery of Victoria; and Ballarat Fine Art Gallery.

HAYNES, GEORGE. (35) Born 1938, East Africa. Studied at Chelsea School of Art, London. Came to Perth, Australia, in 1962 where he now lives. He has had a number of one-man shows especially in Perth and Melbourne. In 1972 he won the William Angliss Prize. He revisited Europe in 1972–73 and spent six months in Paris, a sojourn which both consolidated and expanded his painting. Represented in the Art Gallery of Western Australia and the University of Western Australia.

HICK, JACQUELINE. (102) Born 1920, Adelaide. Studied at South Australian School of Art, Central School of Arts, London, and Fernand Leger Studio, Paris. Returned to Australia 1952; in 1968 studied in Mexico and U.S.A. She has exhibited frequently in group and one-woman shows throughout Australia and has been represented in shows in London, Europe, U.S.A., Indo-China, and India. Represented in all State galleries; National Gallery, Canberra; London Guildhall; and in many regional and private collections.

HODGKINSON, FRANK. (108) Born 1919, Sydney. Studied at East Sydney Technical College and later at the Datillo-Rubbo Atelier. After five years with the Australian Imperial Forces in North Africa and the Pacific, he painted for six years in Europe. He returned to Europe 1959–60, and travelled to U.S.A. 1961. Settled in Spain

1962–68 and returned to Australia in 1970. His many one-man shows include those held throughout Australia and in Madrid, London, New York, and Los Angeles. Represented in most State galleries and widely in private collections in a number of countries.

HOLZNER, ANTON. (44) Born 1935, Innsbruck, Austria. Toured Europe 1962–63 before the first of six one-man shows held since 1963. In 1963 he won the Robin Hood Prize. Represented in the Art Gallery of South Australia; National Gallery, Canberra; National Gallery of Victoria; and in numerous private collections.

HOPKINS, JOHN. (59) Born 1943, Melbourne. Studied at Swinburne Technical College and was a commercial draftsman for the Victorian Railways. His first one-man show was held in 1970 and he was accorded a mini-retrospective during his Creative Arts Fellowship (1973–74) at the Australian National University, Canberra. Represented in the Newcastle City Art Gallery and galleries of Geelong and Ballarat.

HOWLEY, JOHN. (7) Born 1931, Melbourne. Studied at National Gallery School, Melbourne. Settled in Israel 1965; returned to Melbourne 1967. Since 1967 he has been at the Museum of Modern Art and Design, Melbourne; he has had thirteen one-man shows in Sydney, Melbourne, Perth, Tel Aviv, and Jerusalem. Represented in the National Gallery, Canberra; University of Melbourne; National Gallery of Victoria; and in many private collections.

IVANYI, BELA. (68) Born 1936, Hungary. Came to Australia in 1957. He has had a number of one-man shows in Sydney and is noted for the sparse clarity and the subtlety of volume in his work. His most recent exhibition was held in Sydney in 1975.

JACKS, ROBERT. (92) Born 1943, Melbourne. Studied at the Royal Melbourne Institute of Technology. He has had ten one-man shows in Australia, Toronto, and New York City, the last there being in 1973. He has lived in N.Y.C. for the last six years. He was represented in "The Field" Exhibition, National Gallery of Victoria; in the Art Gallery of N.S.W., 1968; and in several State galleries.

JACKSON, ROSS. (110) Born 1939, Sydney. Self-taught. Varied career as journalist, scriptwriter, actor, transport manager, and carpenter. Lived in Europe 1962–68. Since first one-man show in 1969 he has had four others and has participated in significant group shows. In 1972 he won the Mosman Prize and in 1974 the Civic Permanent Award, Canberra.

JAKSIC-BERGER, MIMI. (105) Born in Yugoslavia. Studied at the Technical Institute, Petch, and studied restoration of frescoes. Lived in Paris 1958–59 and came to Australia 1959. Has won over eighty awards and prizes and since her first one-woman show in 1970 she has held ten others. Her work is widely represented in regional, municipal, and private collections.

JAMES, LOUIS. (2) Born 1920, Adelaide. Self-taught. First showed in Adelaide in 1949 then worked for fifteen years in England, exhibiting in London and the provinces. He returned to Australia in 1964. Since 1949 he has had thirty one-man shows in Europe, Melbourne, Sydney, Adelaide, Brisbane, and Newcastle. He has shown in important exhibitions abroad. Represented in public collections in Newcastle-upon-Tyne; Newcastle, N.S.W.; Hull; Leeds; Oxford; the State collections of N.S.W., South Australia, Queensland; in numerous university, college, and regional collections; and in the National Gallery, Canberra.

JAMIESON, GIL. (93) Born 1934, Monto, Queensland. Mainly self-taught. Since 1961 he has had eighteen one-man shows. He is widely represented in many private collections in Sydney, Brisbane, Melbourne, and Rockhampton where he exhibited in 1974 and 1975. Also represented in the National Gallery, Canberra; National Gallery of Victoria; Newcastle City Gallery; and in many collections in Australia and abroad.

JAY, VIRGINIA. (91) Born 1946, Sale, Victoria. Studied at the South Australian School of Art. Overseas study trip in 1963. Since 1969 she has had four one-woman shows in Adelaide, Melbourne, and Sydney and has participated in several significant group shows.

Represented in the National Gallery, Canberra; the State galleries of Tasmania, Western Australia, and Queensland; and four regional galleries in Victoria; as well as in private collections.

JOHNSON, MICHAEL. (71) Born 1938, Sydney. Studied at the Julian Ashton Art School and National Art School, Sydney, 1953–59, and Central School of Art, London, 1961–62. Returned to Australia 1967. Since 1969 has painted in New York City, returning to Australia briefly in 1974 and for a year's teaching in 1975. Since 1967 he has had five one-man shows in Sydney and Melbourne and three in N.Y.C. He has been included in important shows abroad including Australian representation at the Sao Paulo Bienal, 1969. Represented in the National Gallery, Canberra; Art Gallery of N.S.W.; National Gallery of Victoria; Croydon Education Committee, London; Westinghouse U.S.A.; Chase Manhattan Bank, U.S.A.; and widely in private collections.

JORDAN, COL. (95) Born 1935, Sydney. Studied at the University of Sydney and Balmain Teachers' College. Since 1965 he has exhibited regularly, with nine one-man shows since 1966 in Sydney, Canberra, and Melbourne. He has won eight significant prizes since 1965, gained the Flotta Lauro Scholarship in 1971, and studied in Europe and U.S.A. in 1972. Represented in the National Gallery, Canberra; Newcastle City Gallery; Christchurch Gallery, New Zealand; Sydney Teachers' College; and in regional collections.

JUNIPER, ROBERT. (107) Born 1929, Merredin, Western Australia. After studying commercial art and industrial design at Beckenham School of Art, Kent, he returned to Australia where he has had many one-man shows, principally in Western Australia. Represented widely in national and private collections.

KEMP, ROGER. (37) Born 1908, Bendigo, Victoria. Studied at Royal Melbourne Technical College and National Gallery School, Melbourne. Travelled abroad in 1966 and worked in London 1970–72. Since 1945 he has had sixteen one-man shows in Sydney, Melbourne, and London. He has won distinguished prizes: the Georges 1965, the Transfield 1965, the Blake 1968 and 1970, and the Distinguished Artist's Award 1974. He has been included in significant exhibitions abroad: Expo, Canada 1967, "Ten Australians" 1975, and in the Sydney Biennale 1974. Represented in the National Gallery, Canberra; all State and many regional galleries.

KEMPF, FRANZ. (8) Born 1926, Melbourne. Studied at National Art School, Melbourne. Worked in London, Austria, Perugia, 1957–60. Returned to Europe and visited Israel 1965. He has been active as a print-maker since 1954 and in The Contemporary Art Society and the Print Council. Since 1964 he has had twelve one-man shows. Represented in Victoria and Albert Museum, London; Betsalel Museum, Israel; National Gallery, Canberra; most State galleries; regional collections; and in various institutions abroad.

KOSSATZ, LES. (103) Born 1943, Melbourne. Studied Royal Melbourne Institute of Technology. He had his first one-man show in Melbourne in 1967 and has since had four others in Melbourne and Brisbane. He has had a number of commissions for stained glass windows for chapels, churches, galleries, and private homes. In 1975 his *Sheep Sculpture* was shown in Sydney, Melbourne, and Adelaide.

LA GRANGE, FRANZ. (56) Born 1947, Amsterdam. Studied with the painter Jan Korthals and sculptor Szcoura. Since 1968 he has had eight one-man shows in Amsterdam, Utrecht, and Sydney; he has also participated in notable group shows in Basel and Utrecht. Represented in the Power Gallery of Contemporary Art, Sydney, and in private collections in Australia and Holland.

LANCELEY, COLIN. (20) Born 1938, Dunedin, New Zealand. Studied at East Sydney Technical College 1956–60. Member of Annandale (later Imitation) Realist Group. Travelled to Italy in 1965 and lives in London, making periodic visits to Australia. Since 1962 he has had twelve one-man shows in London, Sydney, Adelaide, Melbourne, Cracow, and New York City. He won the Helena Rubinstein Scholarship 1964, Edinburgh Festival Prize 1967, and the Suite of Prints Prize, Cracow 1968. Represented in the National Gallery, Canberra; the State galleries of N.S.W., Victoria, and South Australia; Museum of Modern Art, New York; the Tate

Gallery, London; national museums of Cracow, Warsaw, Poznaw; Kunstverein, Hamburg; and the Stedelijk Museum, Amsterdam.

LARTER, RICHARD. (38) Born 1929, Hornchurch, London. Studied part-time at St Martin's School of Art during the second World War. In 1950 he went to Algiers; in 1952–53 he attended evening classes at Toynbee Hall, London. 1954–57 Shoreditch Teachers' College, Surrey. Group shows in Paris, London, and Moscow, 1957–62. Came to Sydney 1962. Since 1965 he has had ten one-man shows in Sydney. Represented in the National Gallery, Canberra; the State galleries of N.S.W., South Australia, and Western Australia; and in private collections.

LAYCOCK, DONALD. (85) Born 1931, Melbourne. Studied at National Art School, Melbourne. Since 1959 he has had regular one-man shows in Melbourne, Sydney, and Adelaide. Represented Australia in the Sao Paulo Bienal 1969, and was included in the European tour of "Ten Australians" 1975. He won the Travelodge Prize in 1970. Represented in the National Gallery, Canberra; the State galleries of N.S.W., Victoria, and Western Australia; Castlemaine Art Gallery; and Newcastle City Gallery.

LEACH-JONES, ALUN. (5) Born 1937, United Kingdom. Studied at Liverpool College of Art and South Australian School of Art. Since 1964 he has had fifteen one-man shows throughout Australia and in Auckland, Kuala Lumpur, Singapore, and New Delhi. His work has been included in important international exhibitions such as the print biennales of Tokyo, Cracow, and Ljubljana, Yugoslavia. Represented in the Museum of Modern Art, New York; national galleries of Wales, Malaysia, Canberra; all Australian State galleries; in a number of regional and university collections; and in private collections in U.S.A., U.K., Malaysia, and Australia.

LOOBY, KEITH. (3) Born 1940, Sydney. Studied at National Art School, Sydney. Lived abroad, mainly in Italy, 1960–67, when he had his first one-man show in Turin and Rome. Since returning to Australia he has had one-man shows in Sydney, Canberra, Melbourne, Adelaide, Perth, and Newcastle. He has won a number of prizes including the Blake in 1973. He was Creative Arts Fellow at the Australian National University 1973–74. In 1972 he was art critic for the *National Times*. Represented in the National Gallery, Canberra; State galleries of Western Australia, Tasmania, South Australia; and City Gallery, Geelong.

LYNN, ELWYN. (99) Born 1917, Canowindra, N.S.W. B.A., Dip.Ed., F.R.S.A., Awarded Member of the Order of Australia 1975. No formal art training. Travelled in Europe and U.S.A. on seven occasions since 1958, in 1964 on a U.S. State Department Leader Grant. He was editor of the Contemporary Art Society Broadsheet 1955–70, art critic for various papers and journals 1963–72. Author of and contributor to a number of books. Curator, Power Gallery, Sydney University 1969. Associate editor *Quadrant* and *Art International*. Since 1958 he has had many one-man exhibitions in Australia and has been represented in shows abroad. Represented in all State galleries; city galleries of Newcastle and Launceston; several universities and national galleries in New Zealand and Malaysia.

McKAY, BRIAN. (17) Born 1926, Meckering, Western Australia. No formal art training. He has had several one-man shows in Perth, London, Sydney, and Canada. Represented in the State galleries of Western Australia and N.S.W. His first paintings had affinities with Jackson Pollock, but in 1964, working in Greece, France, Morocco, and London he became more interested in the modes of Frank Stella and Joseph Albers. His work is in many private collections in Australia and America.

McLEAN, BRIDGID. (18) Born 1946. Studied at National Art School, East Sydney, completing her diploma course in 1968. Her first one-woman show was in 1973. She won the Cowra Art Prize in 1969, 1970, and 1971.

MAJZNER, VICTOR. (13) Born 1945, Ufa, U.S.S.R. He lived in Paris for a year before coming to Australia where he studied at the Caulfield Institute of Technology. Since 1971 he has had seven one-man shows in Perth, Adelaide, Melbourne, and Brisbane and has participated in a number of important prize and invitational exhibitions, securing six prizes and awards. Represented in city collections of Armidale, Geelong, and Alice Springs; Flinders

University; Queen Victoria Museum, Launceston; and the Tasmanian Museum, Hobart.

MAKIN, JEFFREY. (21) Born 1943, Wagga Wagga. Studied at National Art School, East Sydney. 1972–75 art critic, the *Sun*, Melbourne. Since 1967 he has had twelve one-man shows in Sydney, Melbourne, and Canberra. He has won a number of prizes including the Rockdale and the Drummoyne, 1966, and the Southern Cross Prize in Sydney, 1968.

MATTHEWS, NEVIL. (64) Born 1930, Ayr, Queensland. Studied at Brisbane Art School and with Jon Molvig. Worked in London 1966–67. First one-man show in Brisbane, 1962, was followed by eight others in Brisbane, Sydney, and Melbourne; in 1973 the Ray Hughes Gallery, Brisbane, surveyed ten years of his work. He has had important commissions at the University of Queensland for stained glass windows. Represented in the teachers' colleges of Townsville and Mt Gravatt; National Gallery, Canberra; University of Queensland; James Cook University; Newcastle City Art Gallery; and in private collections in Australia, England, France, Switzerland, U.S.A., and Holland.

MILGATE, RODNEY. (4) Born 1934, Kyogle, N.S.W. Studied at National Art School, East Sydney. Since his first one-man show in Sydney in 1962, he has had ten one-man shows in Sydney, Melbourne, Canberra, and Brisbane. He has won a number of prizes including the Blake 1966 and 1975, and in 1968 a Harkness Scholarship enabled him to study in U.S.A. and Europe. He has been a critic and is an author, poet, and playwright. He has taught variously and extensively and is now with the Mackie College of Advanced Education. Represented in the National Gallery, Canberra; most State galleries; many universities; and in private and public collections in Australia and abroad.

MITELMAN, ALLAN. (96) Born 1946, Poland. Came to Australia in 1953. Studied at Prahran Institute of Technology, Melbourne, and travelled 1969–70 in the Middle East and Europe. Since 1969 he has had eight one-man shows in Melbourne and Brisbane. He has been included in important print shows in Australia and abroad—New Zealand 1971, South America 1974, and Tokyo 1974. Represented in the Museum of Modern Art, New York; city galleries of Auckland, Christchurch, Ballarat, Shepparton, Geelong, and Newcastle; the State galleries of Victoria, Queensland, and N.S.W.

NOLAN, SIDNEY. (29) Born 1917, Melbourne. Studied briefly at the National Gallery School, Melbourne. Since his first one-man show in Melbourne he has had seventy one-man shows and retrospectives in Australia, Rome, London, New York, Aldeburgh, Phoenix, Darmstadt, Oxford, Dublin, Paris, and Newcastle-on-Tyne. He was awarded a C.B.E. in 1963. His first Kelly series was painted in 1946–47. He has lived in London since 1955 and made frequent visits to Australia, U.S.A., and Africa. He has illustrated a number of books, implemented tapestries, and has worked extensively in screenprinting. In 1975 he presented a group of early works for display in Lanyon House, Canberra, and held a further one-man show in London. Represented in the Museum of Modern Art, New York; Tate Gallery, London; National Gallery, Canberra; all State and most regional and university collections.

NOTT, ANDREW. (14) Born 1946, Sydney. Studied Camberwell Art School, London. Lived in London 1959–63 when he returned to Australia. Since 1969 he has had six one-man shows including one of drawings. Travelled to Europe and New York City after he won the Flotta Lauro Scholarship in 1970. He won three art prizes in 1974: Stanthorpe, Townsville, and Lismore. Represented in the National Gallery, Canberra; city galleries of Lismore, Stanthorpe, and Townsville; Macquarie University; and the Art Gallery of N.S.W.

O'DONNELL, TERENCE. (73) Born 1942, Sydney. Studied at the National Art School, East Sydney. In 1967, after winning an English Speaking Union Scholarship, the Park Regis Painting Prize, and Stocks and Holdings Prize, all in 1966, he travelled to Canada where he painted and taught, and to U.S.A., Mexico, Europe, and Nepal. Returned to Australia in 1969. He has had one-man shows in 1971 and 1974 and has participated in a number of thematic exhibitions.

OLDFIELD, ALAN. (55) Born 1943, Sydney. Studied at the National Art School, East Sydney. Since 1966 he has had eight one-man shows in Sydney and Melbourne, and has been included in significant group shows such as "The Field" 1968, "Colour and Structure" 1970, and "Australian Art Today" which toured South-East Asia. He visited Europe and U.S.A. in 1970. He won the Young Contemporaries Prize in 1970 and the Mosman in 1974; also in 1974 he gained a Visual Arts Board grant to work in Italy. Represented in the National Gallery, Canberra; the State galleries of N.S.W., Victoria, and Western Australia; and in Flinders University and private collections.

OLSEN, JOHN. (40) Born 1928, Newcastle, N.S.W. Studied at Julian Ashton Art School and Orban Art School, both in Sydney, and studied and worked later in London, Paris, and Spain. He has lived in Majorca and Portugal and has won a number of important prizes: the Georges, the Perth, and the H. C. Richards. He has made tapestries, painted mural ceilings, and the mural for the Sydney Opera House. He has been included in noted group shows abroad and was in "Direction One," Sydney, 1956. Represented in the National Gallery, Canberra; all State galleries; and extensively in private collections.

OWEN, ROBERT. (76) Born 1937, Sydney. Studied sculpture at National Art School, East Sydney, 1958–62. Lived in Greece, and studied in Turkey and Italy 1963–66. Lived in London, 1966–75, visited New York City 1968 and became involved with constructivism. Since 1965 he has had six one-man shows in Sydney and Melbourne, and has participated in notable group shows in London, Oxford, Birmingham, New York City, and Edinburgh. He was a prize winner in the John Moores exhibition, Liverpool, in 1969. Represented in the Art Gallery of N.S.W.; National Bank of Australia; and in important institutional and private collections.

PEART, JOHN. (22) Born 1945, Brisbane. Studied at Brisbane Technical College Art School. Since his first one-man show in 1967 he has had ten such exhibitions in Melbourne, Sydney, and New Zealand. He has been represented in important group shows, "The Field" 1968, and "Australian Art Today" which was sent to South-East Asia. In 1969 he travelled in U.S.A. and Europe and, after working in England, decided to settle there. He returned briefly to Australia in 1972. Represented in the National Gallery, Canberra; most State galleries; city galleries of Newcastle, Wollongong, Launceston, and Shepparton; and in five university collections.

POWDITCH, PETER. (98) Born 1942, Sydney. Studied at National Art School, East Sydney. Since 1966 he has had eight one-man shows in most capital cities, has been represented in important group shows such as "Recent Australian Art" in the Art Gallery of N.S.W. 1973, and in the Sydney Biennale 1973. He has won a number of prizes—six in 1972 and three in 1974, in which year he visited U.S.A. Represented in the National Gallery, Canberra; the State galleries of N.S.W., Western Australia, Victoria, Tasmania, and South Australia; in the city galleries of Geelong and Newcastle; and widely in private collections.

PROUD, GEOFFREY. (32) Born 1946, Adelaide. First showed in Sydney at Watters Gallery in "Four Painters" 1965. Since 1966 he has had six one-man shows in Sydney, Melbourne, and Perth, the latest being in 1974. His work is in private collections throughout Australia.

PUGH, CLIFTON. (24) Born 1924, Melbourne. Studied at National Gallery School, Melbourne. His first small one-man show at Mirka's Café, Melbourne, was followed by some twenty others throughout Australia and in London, Mexico City, St Louis, and Auckland. In 1973 a retrospective toured the regional galleries of Victoria and in 1974 Melbourne University accorded him a portrait retrospective. He has made murals in various media, participated in films, and has won the Archibald Prize three times. Represented in the national collection; all State galleries; many regional galleries; and in collections in U.S.A., N.Z., and England.

RANKIN, DAVID. (42) Born 1946, Plymouth, England. Self-taught. Came to Australia 1949. Since 1968 he has had eight one-man shows in Sydney and twelve in Brisbane, Melbourne, Canberra, and Adelaide. In 1971 he won the L. J. Harvey and the Ballarat prizes for drawing, the Stanthorpe 1974, and the Maitland 1975.

Represented in the National Gallery, Canberra; the Queensland Art Gallery; city collections of the Gold Coast, Ballarat, Armidale, and Wollongong.

RAPOTEC, STANISLAUS. (51) Born 1913, Yugoslavia. Studied at University of Zagreb. Came to Australia 1948. Since 1952 he has lived in Adelaide, where he first settled, and has had eighteen one-man shows throughout Australia and in London, Paris, and Austria, the last two in 1975. He is at present living in Paris. He has been included in important group shows and won the Blake in 1961. Represented in the National Gallery, Canberra; the State galleries of Queensland, N.S.W., South Australia, and Western Australia; Wellington Gallery, N.Z.; the Vatican Gallery, Rome; and in private collections in U.S.A., England, France, and N.Z.

REES, LLOYD. (74) Born 1895, Brisbane. Studied at Brisbane Technical College and later in London and Rome 1923–24. He has exhibited widely throughout Australia and in London in 1953 and 1973. His memoirs, *Treasures of a Lifetime*, were published in 1969, the year of his retrospective at the Art Gallery of N.S.W. Long active in art organisations, he was awarded an honorary Doctorate of Letters by the University of Sydney in 1970. Represented in the national collection; all State and many regional galleries; and extensively in private collections.

REINHARD, KEN. (28) Born 1936, Mudgee, N.S.W. Studied National Art School, East Sydney, and University of N.S.W. Since 1964 he has had fifteen one-man shows in Sydney, Newcastle, Adelaide, and Melbourne. He has exhibited in important group shows and prize competitions, winning the Marland House Prize in 1971 and subsequently executed a sculpture for Marland House, Melbourne. Represented in the National Gallery, Canberra; the State galleries of N.S.W. and Western Australia; the Newcastle City Gallery; and in many private collections. He is Dean of the Art School, the Alexander Mackie College of Advanced Education.

ROBERTSON-SWANN, RON. (87) Born 1941, Sydney. Studied at National Art School, East Sydney, and at St Martin's School of Art, London. From 1962 he taught and worked in England, mainly in sculpture. He held his first one-man show of paintings and sculpture in Australia in 1968; since then he has had ten such shows including a retrospective at Newcastle City Gallery in 1975 and a show in N.Y.C. in 1971. In England he exhibited in significant group shows. In 1969 he won the Transfield and Comalco prizes, and has been included in important shows touring abroad. Represented in the collections of the Leicestershire Education Authority; National Gallery, Canberra; Mildura Arts Centre; and the State galleries of Victoria and Western Australia.

ROSE, DAVID. (26) Born 1936, Melbourne. Graduated in Science (Forestry), Melbourne and Canberra, 1959. Travelled in Europe 1964–65 and studied print-making in Spain. Since 1961 he has had eighteen one-man exhibitions, has represented Australia in print shows in Poland, India, and U.S.A. He has independently shown in international print exhibitions from 1969 to 1974 in Carpi, Bradford, Ljubljana, Rijeka, Fredrickstad (Norway), and Cracow. Represented in the National Gallery, Canberra; the State galleries of Queensland, Western Australia, South Australia; and in the Museum of Modern Art, N.Y.C.

SANSOM, GARETH. (86) Born 1939, Melbourne. Studied at Royal Institute of Technology, Melbourne. Since 1959 he has had ten one-man shows in Melbourne and Sydney. In 1967 he visited Asia, Europe, and London and in 1971 the West Coast, U.S.A. He has been included in travelling exhibitions to South-East Asia, New Zealand, and U.S.A. Represented in the National Gallery, Canberra; National Gallery of Victoria; Ballarat Fine Art Gallery; Ballarat State College; and in private collections in Australia, U.K., and U.S.A.

SENBERGS, JAN. (11) Born 1939, Riga, Latvia. Studied in Australia and abroad. Since his first one-man show in Melbourne in 1962 he has had six others in that city and in Sydney. In 1973 he represented Australia at the Sao Paulo Bienal and independently exhibited at the biennales of Ljubljana 1965, Tokyo 1966, and Bradford 1969. Represented in the National Gallery, Canberra; the State galleries of N.S.W., Western Australia, South Australia; the

city collections of Newcastle and Ballarat; the Museum of Fine Arts, Houston; and the Chase Manhattan Bank, N.Y.C.

SERELIS, VYTAS. (109) Born 1946, Germany, of Lithuanian parents in transit to Australia. Studied at South Australian School of Art. His first one-man show was in Adelaide in 1967; he has had several others including one at the 1974 Adelaide Festival of Arts. He has been involved in making and playing instruments, illustrating, book production, and studying photography. In 1969 he visited North Africa, Greece, and India. He won the Alice Springs Prize in 1974.

SHANNON, MICHAEL. (101) Born 1927, Kapunda, South Australia. Studied at National Gallery School, Melbourne, and later in Paris with Fernand Leger. Since his first one-man show in Melbourne in 1952, he has exhibited regularly in Melbourne, Sydney, Brisbane, Adelaide, and Perth. In 1953 and 1955 he won the Crouch Prize, Ballarat, and in 1970 the Muswellbrook Prize. He was art critic for the *Australian*, 1973–75. Represented in the National Gallery, Canberra; all State galleries; many regional galleries; the First City National Bank, Boston; and the Monash and Western Australian universities.

SHARP, MARTIN. (15) Born 1942, Sydney. Has had some seven thematic shows in London and Sydney from "Art for Mart's Sake," Sydney 1965 to a mini-retrospective 1952–75, Coventry Gallery, Sydney. Art Director *Oz Magazine* 1963–69. Originator of publications *Magic Theatre Oz* and *Art Book*. Painted Luna Park, North Sydney 1973–75; worked on production of the film *Picnic at Hanging Rock* 1975. Represented in the National Gallery, Canberra; Art Gallery of N.S.W.; Victoria and Albert Museum, London; and in many private collections.

SHEAD, GARRY. (100) Born 1942, Sydney. Studied at North Sydney Technical College. He has had one-man shows since 1966 and since 1962 has produced five films. He won the Young Contemporaries Prize in 1966, visited Europe in 1973, and occupied the Power Studio in Paris. Represented in the South Australian Art Gallery; Mildura Art Gallery; and in private collections.

SIBLEY, ANDREW. (79) Born 1933, Kent, England. Studied at Gravesend School of Art 1946, National Art School, East Sydney 1951, St Martin's School of Art 1953. Came to Australia 1948; settled 1957. In 1972 he returned to Europe, mainly Germany, for a year. He has had twelve one-man shows in Sydney, Brisbane, Perth, and Melbourne between 1961 and 1974 and has won numerous prizes including the Transfield and the Tasmanian Art Gallery prizes. Represented in the National Gallery, Canberra; all State galleries; a number of university collections; and in many private collections in Australia and abroad.

SMART, JEFFREY. (106) Born 1921, Adelaide. Studied at South Australian School of Art and later in Europe, including a period with Fernand Leger. He has had many one-man shows including fourteen from 1957 to 1974 in Sydney and Melbourne; since 1965 he has exhibited regularly in London and Italy where he lives. He has been included in noted group exhibitions abroad and is represented in the National Gallery, Canberra; most State galleries; city galleries of Ballarat and Newcastle; Yale and Sydney universities; and in many private collections in England, Italy, and Australia.

SMITH, ERIC. (25) Born 1919, Melbourne. Trained in commercial art, 1936–37, and at Melbourne Technical College 1947–51. Since 1951 he has had fourteen one-man shows in Sydney and Melbourne and has won many prizes including the Wynne, the Sulman, and the Blake on five occasions, and various portrait awards. He showed with "Direction One," Sydney 1956. He has carried out commissions for mosaics and stained glass windows, has shown in group exhibitions abroad, and is represented in the National Gallery, Canberra; most State galleries; and extensively in private collections.

STANNAGE, MIRIAM. (75) Born 1939, Northam, Western Australia. No formal art training; travelled and studied in England, Europe, and Canada. In 1971 she worked in the Power Studio, Paris. She has had a number of one-woman shows in Perth, and in Sydney in 1974, in which year she was a Georges Prize purchase. Represented in Art Gallery of Western Australia; the University of

Western Australia; and the Power Gallery of Contemporary Art, the University of Sydney.

STORRIER, TIM. (97) Born 1949, Sydney. Studied at National Art School, East Sydney. In 1969 he held a two-man show in Sydney and in the same year his first one-man show in Melbourne. Since then he has had three one-man shows. In 1972 he toured U.S.A., Europe, and the Middle East; in 1973 he toured Central Australia and in 1975 visited Lake Eyre. He was included in the Expo '74, Spokane, U.S.A., exhibition and is represented in the State galleries of N.S.W. and Western Australia; the National Gallery, Canberra; and in many private collections.

SZABO, JOSEPH. (69) Born 1932, Budapest. Came to Australia in 1949. Studied at the National Art School, East Sydney. Since 1962 he has had ten one-man shows in Sydney and Melbourne and exhibited in "The Field" exhibition at the Art Gallery of N.S.W. and the National Gallery of Victoria in 1968. Represented in the National Gallery, Canberra; Art Gallery of N.S.W.; Mosman Municipal Council; and in private collections.

TAYLOR, MICHAEL. (57) Born 1933, Sydney. Studied at the National Art School, East Sydney, and in Melbourne. In 1958 he travelled in India and from 1960 to 1963 in Europe. He had his first one-man show in Sydney in 1963 and exhibited in Sydney, Tasmania, Melbourne, and Adelaide between 1964 and 1975. In 1975 he travelled to N.Y.C., India, and Europe. He represented Australia in the Young Painters' Biennale in Paris, 1963, and in the Triennale, India, 1975. Represented in the National Gallery, Canberra; Art Gallery of N.S.W.; and in many private collections.

TUCKER, ALBERT. (94) Born 1914, Melbourne. Worked in England, France, Italy, Germany, U.S.A. 1947–60. He has had one-man shows throughout Australia, in Amsterdam, Paris, Rome, London, New York City, and Mexico City. He has been included in group shows in Venice, Ireland, Canada, Japan, and Brazil. Represented in the National Gallery, Canberra; all State galleries; regional galleries; Museum of Modern Art, N.Y.C.; the Solomon R. Guggenheim Museum, N.Y.C.; and in many private collections in Australia and abroad.

TYNDALL, PETER. (63) Born 1951, Melbourne. Studied Architecture, Melbourne University and Royal Melbourne Institute of Technology. He held his first one-man show in Melbourne in 1972 and his third in 1974, in which year he won the Darnell de Gruchy Prize, the University of Queensland. He has shown in a number of group exhibitions such as "Boxes" and "Survival Kits," both at the National Gallery of Victoria. Artist-in-residence, Monash University 1975. Represented in the University of Queensland; regional galleries; and in private collections.

UPWARD, PETER. (34) Born 1932, Melbourne. Studied at Julian Ashton Art School, Sydney. Returned to Melbourne, then settled in Sydney in 1960. In 1962 he went to London where he exhibited in 1962, 1964, and 1971. His earlier work was again shown in Sydney in 1972 and since his return to Australia he has had three more one-man shows. Represented in the National Gallery, Canberra; several State galleries; and in private collections in England and Australia.

WALLACE-CRABBE, ROBIN. (54) Born 1938, Melbourne. Studied at Royal Melbourne Institute of Technology. Since his first one-man show in 1963 he has had others in Sydney, Melbourne, Canberra, and Adelaide. He has written art criticism and has exhibited in group shows of Australian prints in Cracow and Washington, D.C. Represented in the National Gallery, Canberra; Art Gallery of South Australia; the universities of Melbourne, Adelaide, and Brisbane; and in private collections.

WALLIS, CHRISTOPHER. (77) Born 1947, Sydney. Studied at National Art School, East Sydney. He lived in London from 1969 for a number of years designing textiles and interiors, and was commissioned to do murals. He had his first one-man show in 1973 on his return to Australia and two others, also in Sydney, in 1974 and 1975.

WARREN, GUY. (84) Born 1921, Goulburn, N.S.W. Studied at National Art School, East Sydney, and Chelsea and Central schools of art, London. He has lived in London since 1959 and has held eighteen one-man shows throughout Australia. He has participated in significant group shows abroad such as Expo '67, Montreal. He won the Perth Festival Prize, the Flotta Lauro Travelling Scholarship in 1967, and the Georges Prize in 1974. Represented in the National Gallery, Canberra; most State galleries; regional and university collections; and the Contemporary Art Society, London.

WATKINS, DICK. (70) Born 1937, Sydney. Studied at Julian Ashton School, Sydney 1955–58 and East Sydney Technical College 1958. Studied and worked in Europe 1959–61 and again in 1974–75. Since 1963 he has had twelve one-man shows in Sydney and Canberra, which included two retrospectives, one in Sydney in 1969 and the other in Canberra in 1973. He has been included in notable group shows such as the Transfield, Georges, Recent Australian Art in the Art Gallery of N.S.W., and "The Field," 1968. Represented in the National Gallery, Canberra; several State galleries; and widely in private collections in Australia and abroad.

WESTWOOD, BRYAN. (81) Born 1930, Lima, Peru. Came to Australia 1950. Studied in Rio de Janeiro and National Art School, East Sydney. Visited U.S.A. 1943–49; lived in Rome, 1968, and in France, 1974. Since 1969 he has had eight one-man shows in Adelaide, Sydney, and Melbourne. Represented in the National Gallery, Canberra; Art Gallery of Western Australia; Queen's Hall, Canberra; and in private collections.

WILLIAMS, FRED. (89) Born 1927, Melbourne. Studied at National Gallery School, Melbourne, and later at Chelsea Art School, London. Since 1956 he has had one-man shows of paintings and etchings throughout Australia. He has won important prizes such as the Transfield, the Georges, the Helena Rubinstein Scholarship, and the McCaughey Prize. Represented in the National Gallery, Canberra; all State galleries; Museum of Modern Art, N.Y.C.; the Victoria and Albert Museum, London; and extensively in private collections.

WHISSON, KENNETH. (112) Born 1927, Lilydale, Victoria. Studied with Danila Vassilieff at Warrandyte 1945–46. Travelled in Europe 1954–56 and in North Africa, the Middle East, Asia, and Europe 1968–70. He has had one-man shows periodically in Melbourne, Sydney, and once in Brisbane. Represented in several State galleries and numerous private collections.

WHITELEY, BRETT. (72) Born 1939, Sydney. Studied at the Julian Ashton Art School, Sydney. He has lived in London, Fiji, and New York City where he painted and exhibited. His first one-man show was held in London in 1962, and since then he has had twenty such shows. In group shows he has exhibited in Holland, Germany, France, Canada, Suva, Spokane, and in the Pittsburgh International. In 1967 he gained a Harkness Fellowship, one of many significant awards. Represented in London in the Tate Gallery, the Contemporary Art Society, and the Victoria and Albert Museum; all Australian State galleries; and the National Gallery, Canberra; also in the Museum of Modern Art, N.Y.C.; Musée d'Art Moderne, Paris; Sao Paulo Museum, Brazil; Museum of Twentieth Century Art, Vienna.